Andre Calbert

Puggles

Everything About Purchase, Care,
Nutrition, Behavior, and Training

Filled with Full-color Photographs by Chelle Calbert
Illustrations by Pam Tanzey

BARRON'S

CONTENTS

THE PUGGLE: WHAT IS IT?

The Puggle is a relatively new hybrid. It is a cross between a purebred female Beagle and a purebred male Pug. The Puggle is an adorable, sweet-tempered, wrinkle-faced, loyal dog that makes a fantastic candidate as a family pet. To understand the Puggle requires briefly looking at its ancestors, the Pug and Beagle.

The Pug: An Ancient Breed

The origin of the Pug is generally accepted to be ancient China. Descriptions of Pugs appear in literature dating back as far as 1000 B.C. During that period, all treasures—including jade, pearls, fine art, dogs, and rare animals—were considered imperial property. The Pugs were the house pets of the emperors and people of nobility. They were presented as gifts of significant value to the rulers of Japan and other countries. During the late sixteenth century, sailors from several European countries began bringing Pugs back to their home countries.

The Netherlands is the first place that the Pug gained wide popularity in the West. Legend has it that in 1572, a Pug was the first to alert King William the Silent of Holland of an enemy attack on their camp by the Spanish, before any Dutch

The Puggle's history dates back to ancient China.

soldier was even aware. In the years following that incident, the Pug became the honored pet of the ruling house of the Dutch and can be seen in many pieces of their artwork. These works of art featured both fawn and black Pugs, which are the two currently recognized colors.

In 1672, Prince William of England brought back some fawn Pugs from Holland during one of his visits. He made public appearances with his Pugs draped in orange ribbons in honor of the House of Orange. Queen Victoria was also known to have had a Pug. She owned a black Pug that was marked with white and was believed to be of Chinese origin. During this period, the black Pugs were not held in much favor and were often removed from the litter and not spoken of. Not until 1876 were black Pugs acknowledged and placed into competition. This is because of the well-born English Lady Brassey, a lover of Pugs and renowned world traveler. In 1876, she brought back several

early years of the twentieth century, the Pug was becoming quite popular in America. The primary goal of the early American breeders was to breed Pugs that could win dog shows across the Atlantic in England and to continue improving on the desired qualities. During World War I, the popularity of the Pug began to dwindle. In 1931, the Pug Dog Club of America was established and became a member of the American Kennel Club. Since that time, the Pug has steadily increased in popularity.

Today the Pug is known to be a superb companion. The colors include black and light to dark fawn. As a toy breed, the Pug is compact. It has a black mask and short muzzle. The black color does not usually have any other markings. The Pug easily adapts to most living environments and prefers to be in the company of its owner. For exercise, the Pug prefers a low-impact morning or an evening stroll. The Pug loves to be pampered and will definitely return the love to its owner. The Pug has an above-average intelligence and prefers to know what is going on at all times. This dog is known for its stable temperament and its loyalty. Many of these desirable traits can be found in the Puggle.

black Pugs from China, who then made a significant impact on the bloodlines in England.

In 1886, Lady Brassey had the bright idea of exhibiting her Chinese blacks at a dog show, where they gained much popularity. This led to many kennels beginning to specialize in blacks and also interbreeding blacks with fawns. This interbreeding is a wide practice that is still in existence today.

The American Pug

The first Pug of record in the United States was a dog by the name of Roderick. It was bred in England of champion lineage and was born July 12, 1878. Not until 1885 did the American Kennel Club recognize the Pug breed. In the

History of the Beagle

Some believe that the origin of the Beagle may belong to ancient Greece. A Greek dictionary written during the second century mentions the use of canines for hunting around 1300 B.C. However, the primary development of the Beagle breed is generally accepted to have occurred in England. The Beagle is believed to have existed in England before the Roman occupation. Historical evidence shows that the Beagle was already established as a hunting dog during the time of the Crusades. The actual origin of the name Beagle in not known. However, the first English literary mention of the Beagle, by name, was published in 1475 in the *Esquire of Iow Degree*.

The Beagle is a scenthound that was bred primarily to hunt hare. There was, and still is, a term used called "Beagling" in which a pack of Beagles would go out on the hunt. Hare hunting was popular as early as the fourteenth century in England. Hunting had become a popular sporting pastime of the wealthy aristocracy, and the Beagle was the dog of choice. The hunter would take the Beagles to an area believed to be inhabited by hare and release them. Once a Beagle picked up on the scent, it would start to sing and was allowed to work the scent. The hunter would then position himself in the area where the hare would most likely end up coming out. Foxes are another small vermin that were hunted by more agile Beagles and Foxhounds.

The Beagle is also called a miniature Foxhound. The markings of some Beagles are identical to that of the Foxhound, but the Foxhound is a larger and faster dog. Many believe that the lineage of the two dogs is intermixed and that both were developed about the same time. In 1861, *The Manual of British Sports* divided the Beagles into four distinct categories: the medium Beagle, dwarf or lapdog Beagle, fox Beagle, and the rough-coated Beagle. These dogs varied in size, speed, markings, and purpose. To this day, you will find many shapes, sizes, and colors of Beagles around the globe. To go into more detail on the different classes of Beagles is beyond the scope of our purpose

Beagles are very popular in the United States.

here. There are many good books available on the subject of Beagles should you require further study.

The Beagle was eventually imported to the United States but kept a low profile. The early American Beagles were considerably smaller than and not as attractive as their English counterparts. The improvement of the American Beagle began around the 1870s when General Richard Rowett of Illinois began importing some excellent breeding stock from the best packs in England. The American Kennel Club (AKC) registered their first Beagle in 1885. General Rowett and a few other fanciers eventually founded the National Beagle Club in 1888, and the breed standard was accepted that same year. During the 1940s and 1950s, the sport of Beagling and the AKC registrations began to grow exponentially. Beagle clubs began to pop up all over the country. Some Beagles would be entered in local-level AKC field trials as well as breed standard bench shows. Some Beagles were even good enough to win both types of competitions to earn the coveted title of Dual Champion.

The Beagle Today

Today's Beagle is still a very popular dog in America. Countless clubs sponsor shows, beagling, and field trials. Beagles have also done quite well in obedience trials. Because of their great sense of smell, small stature, and great disposition, Beagles have been successfully used by the United States Department of Agriculture (USDA) for some time now. These Beagles are part of the USDA's Beagle Brigade and are used at international airports to sniff out illegal and prohibited foodstuffs and plants

that might introduce unwanted diseases into America. They are also used by U.S. Customs to sniff out contraband in luggage and other mailed packages. The Customs agents like the Beagles because the dog can fit into tight spaces and do not intimidate passengers. Another use of the Beagle is by law enforcement personnel to sniff out arson accelerants at the location of a suspicious fire.

Until fairly recently, the majority of Beagle breeders would breed for show or for field trials. Most serious breeders were not breeding Beagles for the sake of selling puppies as pets. That does not mean that there are not plenty of Beagles as pets around the country. On the contrary, many novice breeders have been producing great family pets for a number of years. A great many of the pets also come from serious breeders who have puppies they feel will not make the grade as either show or breeding dogs. Beagles have earned a well-deserved reputation as a wonderful companion and family dog. Because of their breeding history, they are adaptable in many environments ranging from hot to cold and from wet to dry. They are faithful, playful, and loyal dogs who will provide their owners many years of unconditional, loving admiration. These qualities make Beagles such a desirable mix for the Puggle.

Origin of the Puggle

In 1992, a breeder in Wisconsin by the name of Wallace Havens had the idea of breeding a hybrid dog using a Pug and a Beagle. Wallace had already been breeding hybrids for many

The adult size of a Puggle is mostly determined by how large its Beagle mother was.

Puppies this cute are hard to resist.

years and purebreds for about 25 years. A few years earlier, he had spoken to a man that came to his kennel to buy a Cockapoo (Cocker Spaniel/Poodle mix). The gentleman told him that he once had a Pug and Beagle mixed dog and then went on and on about how great of a dog it was and how much he loved it. Wallace kept this in the back of his mind and finally decided to move forward with the hybrid.

As an experienced breeder, Wallace was familiar with both breeds. He determined that the temperament and qualities of the two breeds were quite desirable and would probably have the makings of a good family pet. The puppies from the first litter were so adorable

with their wrinkled foreheads, floppy hound ears, and big, beautiful eyes that Wallace was sure that others would feel the same way. At first, these new dogs did not get a warm reception from the public and were difficult to sell. People would often call Wallace and ask what kind of puppies he had available. When he would tell them that he had a Pug and Beagle mix, he would often get laughs and comments like, "I don't think I want anything like that."

Wallace persisted. He was sure that eventually people would come around and realize what a wonderful a dog this was. He also decided that it needed a name, and the logical choice was the Puggle. Wallace was the first to

These Puggles are self-assured and attentive.

come up with the name and was also the first to register the Puggle with the American Canine Hybrid Club.

Characteristics of the Puggle

The Puggle is a pleasure to live with and a delight to own. One of its most endearing qualities is that it desires to be in your company just as much as you do its company. The Puggle wants to be a loyal friend and strives to please its owner. The Puggle needs to feel like it is an integral part of the family's life. It is a social dog that will gladly share the company of any family member or friend. Although the Puggle is happy to give affection to other family mem-

bers, it may, at times, demand attention from the one who feeds it or pays the most attention to it. Being a perceptive breed, the Puggle easily tunes into its family's daily routine, habits, desires, idiosyncrasies, and expectations. If anything is out of place or the routine changes, the Puggle will immediately recognize the difference and may give you a look or even bark in protest. If it senses you are upset, it may attempt to comfort you by snuggling up next to you. At bedtime, the Puggle prefers to sleep with its owner if allowed to but can easily adapt to a bed of its own or a crate.

Peronality: Self-assured and attentive, the Puggle carries itself with a sort of cocky confidence yet has a friendly and sensitive nature. Protective of its house and family, the Puggle will do its best to alert all family members of an intruder. Being an excellent communicator, the Puggle will have various barks and whines to convey what it is feeling and trying to express. If looking out a window, the bark will be different when another dog is walking by than when a neighbor or other familiar person walks by. If you do something the Puggle does not agree with, it may bark rapidly in succession or snort in protest to alert you of its disapproval. Over time you will learn to distinguish the various barks, howls, and other noises. This will, of course, vary from dog to dog. Incidentally, the need to howl is significantly lessened in the Puggle as compared with the Beagle.

Appetite: A Puggle has quite a hearty appetite and is not very picky about what it eats. In fact, it rarely gets full and believes that more of just about anything is probably better. This can be a detriment to its weight, so you must monitor your Puggle's intake carefully.

Because of its extrakeen sense of smell, the Puggle is aware of most edible things that are within range. Do not be fooled into thinking the coast is clear if you see your Puggle sleeping on its bed. For the Puggle, the next meal is of prime importance. The desire for a snack will usually overcome any feeling of fatigue or laziness. The Puggle is also quite aware of its surroundings and uses cunning and intelligence to assist in figuring out a way to get to some food. If you walk away and leave food on the kitchen table within reach, do not be surprised if you come back to find some scraps on your plate. If you have left a chair pulled out, your Puggle will know. You can expect to find the

Be sure your cupboards are secure or you may come home to a mess.

PUGGLE DETAILS

1. Durable and hardy
2. Will roughhouse with children
3. A loving companion
4. Enjoys snuggling and being a lapdog
5. Typically fawnish tan with a black muzzle
6. Often has a curly tail
7. Averages 14–25 pounds (6.4–11.4 kg)
8. Usually 13–15 inches (33–38 cm) high at the shoulders

dog up on the table devouring anything you have left. It is best to teach your Puggle early not to expect any table scraps from you at dinnertime. All Puggles are fast learners and will always expect a handout if you do it even once. If you have a cat, be sure to leave its food out of reach, as you can be sure the Puggle is aware of its location.

This Puggle pup represents a hardy breed that boasts high energy and low maintenance.

Puggle Variations

Because this is a mixed breed and the Beagle comes in many shapes and sizes, the Puggle can come with various physical characteristics. A Puggle will generally have an elongated snout that eliminates much of the breathing problems and physical limitations associated with the Pug's short muzzle. The Puggle will often inherit more of the stamina and agility present in the Beagle. Because of this, the Puggle can go on longer walks without becoming winded, go for a jog, and run around at the park. It is happy to play fetch with a ball, especially if a treat is involved.

Temperature concerns: The Puggle is generally a hardy dog that can become acclimated in most environments. Some can, however, be born with a shorter muzzle and come with a more compact body. If this is the case, then a little more care may be required. Try not to let your Puggle outside for extended periods of time if the temperature is over 80–85°F (26.7–29.4°C), because it can overheat more easily. Also, if you live in a hotter climate, try to exercise your dog in the early morning or evening. This type of Puggle may also have more of a tendency to snore or snort from time to time.

Coloring: The standard Puggle generally has a tanlike fawn coloring and a slightly curled tail. It also comes in all black or black with white on the paw or under the belly. In rare cases, the Puggle has been known to have some variations of black and tan. Because the black gene is present in most Pug lines, the coloring can vary within the same litter.

Shedding does occur in the Puggle breed and will usually take place twice a year. This will happen once in the spring and then again in the fall. Being a low-maintenance dog, the

Cunning: If you have a gate that restricts the Puggle from accessing certain areas of your home, make sure it is closed behind you as you enter that area. The Puggle will learn the sound the gate makes when it is clicked shut and will attempt to pull the gate open if it does not hear the gate shut properly. You can expect the same for kitchen cabinets where you may store your garbage receptacle. Installing childproof locks may be a good idea. Keep in mind that these tendencies will vary from dog to dog, but the behaviors described here are not uncommon.

Here is a black Puggle with his fawn friends.

Puggle does not require regular grooming. However, you should brush its coat from time to time. This will assist in minimizing the shedding coat from getting all over your clothes and furniture.

Eye discharge: From the Pug, the Puggle may occasionally have some form of eye discharge. A small amount of discharge in the corner of the eye is normal but will not be present in most Puggles. If your Puggle does have discharge, wipe the area with a warm, wet cloth a few times a week. This will prevent the buildup from causing an infection.

Sense of smell: For most Puggles, the nose is a big part of their driving force. While going for walks, you must be prepared for the Puggle to be led by its keen sense of smell. Even if your Puggle has the shorter muzzle, you can expect its face to be stuck to the ground the majority of the time. Be aware of what is on your path. If you are walking in public, keep an eye out for discarded litter, especially if it contains any kind of foodstuffs. Your Puggle will not hesitate to eat a quick snack it might find. The Puggle gets much pleasure from exploring the many fascinating scents along the way. Like the Beagle, this is how it experiences the world. The Puggle can pick up on scents that are a few weeks old. This can draw your dog in a direction other than you intended. Do not be surprised if your Puggle follows an invisible trail that leads you to an unexpected article on the other end. The Puggle has the ability to pick up on specific scents in the presence of other strong odors that for humans would eliminate our ability to smell anything else.

FINDING A GOOD PUGGLE

Once you have decided that a Puggle is right for you, you will have to make many choices to find the perfect dog. Educate yourself before actually searching for your wonderful, new companion.

Are You Prepared?

Unfortunately, after living with a dog for a while, some impulsive buyers realize that the daily requirements of being a new dog owner are more than they bargained for. The initial novelty of having a cute puppy wears off, and dealing with the once-joyous arrival becomes a daily nightmare. The puppy then suffers when it is either abandoned or placed into a shelter by a frustrated owner. This sad scenario happens more often than you may think. The reality is that it could have been avoided in most cases if the owner had done a little homework.

The more informed you are, the more likely you are to anticipate and be equipped to handle the daily ups and downs of owning a puppy. The hope is that everyone else in the house is also willing to do his or her part in

Choosing the right puppy may take some time.

raising and caring for the new Puggle. You must inform other family members about what you've learned because the chances are pretty good that they are as uninformed as you may have been initially. You should ask yourself several questions before purchasing any dog.

Question 1: What are the grooming and hygiene requirements of the Puggle? Is this something that I am willing to do, or will I need to hire a groomer or take my dog to the veterinarian for certain procedures?

Question 2: Am I willing to commit to the daily responsibility that comes with owning a dog for its entire life? A Puggle can live 10–15 years.

Question 3: Do I have another animal like a large dog or jealous cat that could potentially injure my new puppy? If so, have I made the necessary preparations to protect my new puppy? The bite of a larger dog or the swipe of a jealous cat's claw can easily injure the young Puggle.

Be sure to include the children in the daily responsibilities.

CAUTION!
Will Your Family Really Help?

Before getting a new dog, determine if your family members are really ready to care for it. The thought of owning a dog often causes people to make promises that they will later break when the novelty of the new dog wears off. You may hear, "If we get a Puggle, I'll feed him," or "I promise to train and play with him," or "I'll take him for walks." However, if your family members do not live up to their promises, you will still have to feed, train, play with, and walk your four-legged companion. Are you willing and able to shoulder the responsibility?

Question 4: Are you and everyone else in your family committed to raising and caring for the new puppy in your house?

Question 5: Do you have unrealistic expectations in regards to potty training? Some people believe they can housebreak a dog in a couple of weeks. The reality is that it averages 5–6 months for your dog to have some control and up to a year for the dog to totally be trusted alone.

Question 6: Do you have the financial means to provide adequate care for your new Puggle and make sure that it has what it needs? Your Puggle will need collars, leashes, crates, dog beds, toys, shots, flea control, grooming tools, and so on. These things all cost money, and many of them can get destroyed by your puppy, which means an additional expense.

Question 7: Can you provide the care needed and make reasonable accommodations as your dog ages?

Question 8: Are you counting on your children to give the puppy the care and time it needs? Children are notorious for promising to help only to lose interest a week later, leaving you to pick up the slack.

Making the commitment: You must ask yourself these questions before you begin searching for a puppy. By asking yourself these questions and being honest, you are taking a first step in the right direction. At least one person in your household must be willing to commit to the care of the new Puggle. Although puppies can be very entertaining and cute, much effort must be made in the early years to get the dog off to a good start. It

It can be hard to pick from so many cute puppies.

needs to be trained to learn what is expected of it. Your dog must also receive basic obedience training to learn what its boundaries are. This initial training will require a certain level of patience as well as a large portion of your time. If you are committed to all of the things mentioned in this section, then you are off to a great start and will be rewarded by gaining a wonderful companion.

Where Do I Begin My Search?

Your first instincts will be to check with your local pet store or maybe to check out the ads in your daily newspaper. What you may not know is that the Puggle can be difficult to find locally because it is a relatively new mixed breed. Depending on where you live, using these sources may not be the best way to begin your search. Ironically, since the Puggle is a modern mixed breed, it can most easily be found using modern technology. The Internet is probably going to be your best chance of finding a Puggle initially. If you are not familiar with how to search on the Internet, then perhaps you have a friend or family member who can help you. The Internet has many choices and sources for locating a breeder or pet store that may be near you. Maybe you will get lucky and find a Puggle that is right for you at the local shelter as well. There is also a national registry for hybrid dogs that can be found in the resource section at the end of this book. Each source has its advantages and

Do Your Homework

1. Remember—your Puggle will be your responsibility. Will you be able to care for the dog throughout its entire life—from puppyhood all the way to old age?
2. Decide if you will go to a pet store, specialty breeder, shelter, or commercial breeder or if you will use online sources.
3. Have a list of questions ready to determine if you have chosen the right source.
4. What type of puppy do you want? Should it be shy, playful, or aggressive? Should you just base your decision simply on how the dog looks?
5. What time of year should you get your Puggle?
6. How old should your Puggle be when you take it home?

Choosing your puppy in person is the best option.

potential disadvantages, which will be covered in more detail.

Pet Stores

Pet stores have been around for decades, and many people have gotten good-quality pets from these establishments. The key is to speak with the owner and try to find out if the pet store has a screening process for its sources of dogs. You will also want to see if they stand by their puppies and offer a warranty that covers any congenital defects. If you have some dialogue in person, you may get a sense if the owner cares about the animals or is just interested in turning a profit.

A small pet store is a good place to start because the owner may be more hands-on. You may want to avoid a larger pet store that may deal with multiple breeds and may be obtaining their puppies from a dog broker. Because many brokers deal with a large volume, the puppy may not be properly socialized, vaccinated, or dewormed. There is always a risk when you cannot see the facility from which the puppy is coming, but that does not mean you cannot get a quality Puggle from a pet store. You just need to gather as much information as you can about their sources.

Specialty Breeders

Dog breeders come in many forms. Some are big commercial breeders who produce multiple breeds and have hundreds of dogs in their breeder stock. (These are discussed later.) Some are medium-sized breeders who breed a few different breeds. Some are backyard breeders who

These littermates are on the same sleeping schedule.

produce only a few litters a year. Some are specialty breeders who focus on producing only show-quality dogs. More than likely, if you are getting your Puggle from a breeder, it will be from a medium-sized breeder. Commercial breeders mostly sell directly to brokers and pet stores, specialty breeders mostly produce pure-breds, and backyard breeders may not have a Puggle available when you are ready. Keep in mind that most of the breeders in the United States are located in the middle of the country, and you may have difficulty finding one if you live in the coastal states. However, their numbers are starting to grow as the demand increases.

Shelters

Dog shelters can be a great place to locate a Puggle if you live near a big city with a large population. This will statistically increase your chances of finding a Puggle at a shelter. Many shelters run ads featuring their dogs in local newspapers as well as on many Internet sites. They will usually get a nonprofit discount from the newspapers and run big ads with great-looking pictures. Do not let the fact that it is a shelter give you the impression that something is wrong with the dog. You would be surprised at the many reasons that people leave their dogs at the shelter:

1. The dog jumped on people.
2. The dog chewed and barked too much.
3. The dog dug holes in the new grass.
4. The dog liked to roll around in the mud and smelled bad.
5. The dog was too active for my lifestyle.
6. Someone in the family was allergic to the dog.
7. The family had to move away.

Make sure your Puggle comes from a Beagle female and Pug male mix.

Most of the problems, if there are any, can be easily fixed with some basic training. As you can see, many dogs end up at the shelter through no fault of their own and many times do not really have any problems at all. So keep shelters in mind when searching for a dog, and you just might come across what you are hoping for.

Online Sources

Since the creation of the Internet, locating a dog has become much easier. Many sources of dogs can be found on the Web. If you are having trouble locating a reputable source for your Puggle locally, you will need to consider making a long-distance purchase. You can do this by either having it shipped to you or by taking a trip to go and pick up your dog yourself. Many dog breeders now have web sites where you can see pictures of the current puppies that they have available. Many times they will have pictures and testimonials of previous litters that you can see. Often times they will have pictures of their facilities, the breeding stock they use and other helpful information. Many pet stores are also available online these days. They will often have a retail location as well as the ability to ship elsewhere. The next source can be an online pet store that works with reputable breeders to locate the puppy for you. This is a great service because they do a lot of the pre-screening of the breeders and can provide you with the background information, shot records, American Canine Hybrid Club (ACHC) registration, shipping arrangements, and so on. Many breeders do not have the know-how to adapt to this new way of selling. Instead, they rely on various services to assist with many of these tasks.

We recommend that you visit the web site *DesignerDoggies.com* when doing your initial search. Finally, you can usually get a list of breeders from the ACHC at *achclub.com*. This is the main registry for mixed breeds like Puggles.

Commercial Breeders or Puppy Mills

First of all, not all commercial breeders that produce a large volume of dogs are considered puppy mills. This is a myth perpetuated by the animal rights movement in order to win your sympathy and collect donations. A small percentage of bad apples out there give the legitimate breeders a bad name. In contrast, the majorities of commercial breeders care about their puppies and have an adequate staff that helps to ensure that their puppies receive the proper care, socialization, and vaccinations. The dogs that come from these kennels can make wonderful pets, and this source should not be discounted. These large breeders mainly sell their puppies to brokers and pet stores directly, so it is unlikely that you will get a puppy here. However, if you get one from a pet store then there is a good chance it has come from one of these facilities.

Puggles may be registered with the American Canine Hybrid Club.

It is a little-known fact that the majority of commercial breeders in the United States are located in the Midwest and produce most of the dogs for the rest of the country. This region is also known as the Great Plains states and the heartland. Producing puppies is often a time-consuming and thankless job that many breeders work tirelessly at to ensure that their litters are of the highest quality. Little is mentioned about the breeders who are up until the wee hours of the night assisting a dam (female) that is having a difficult time with her delivery or the early stages of motherhood, only to lose one or more of her pups.

Reasons for Choosing Different Puggle Sources

Source	Reasons
Pet stores	• Close to your home • You can often speak directly with the owner
Specialty breeders	• Usually offer warranty to cover congenital defects • Screen all potential owners • Can provide you with American Canine Hybrid Club (ACHC) registration forms, vaccination records, and lineage information • The animal will be properly vaccinated, socialized, and dewormed • Breed their animals for the betterment of the breed, not just to make money
Shelters	• Usually not expensive • The animal will probably be properly vaccinated, socialized, and dewormed
Online sources	• Useful when local sources are unavailable • May be able to provide you with ACHC registration forms, vaccination records, lineage information, and shipping arrangements
Commercial breeders or puppy mills	• Puggles are usually available at all times (however, will often not sell to individuals but only to pet stores) • Will probably provide adequate care, socialization, and vaccinations

This can be very disheartening for the breeder who deeply cares for the mother and her offspring. Many commercial breeders are in the business to make money, but that doesn't mean it is at the expense of quality.

What to Look For in a Source

Because the Puggle is not a purebred, you do not have to be concerned with terms like championship lines or breed standard. These dogs are created to be pets. Those terms give no indication of temperament or intelligence, which are what make a great family pet. Therefore, you need not be concerned with getting caught up in the typical purebred or show dog terminology. What you want to look for is consistency in the traits coming from your prospective breeder. Make sure that the dam is a registered, purebred, female Beagle and the sire is a registered purebred Pug. These new Puggle litters will often be registered with the ACHC. This will help ensure that you are getting predictable results. Some backyard breeders are mating Puggles together. These are called second generation Puggles, and the results are unpredictable. So these breeders are not your best choice.

Seeing Is Believing

If you have your choice, the best place to start would be to visit a breeder who breeds Puggles and see the sire and dam of the litter. It is not uncommon for the male to live elsewhere. Many breeders will take their female to a male that has the quality that they are looking for. This practice is common throughout the dog breeding world and is not breed specific.

The dam should be clean, friendly, and outgoing. If she seems uncomfortable, has aggressive behavior, or tries to hide from you, you may want to pass. However, if the litter is young and the mom happens to be with them while you are there, she will display aggressive behavior and may growl as a sign of protectiveness over her young. This is a normal reaction, and you can overlook it in that case.

The breeder: You want to gather as much information about the breeder and the history of his or her dogs as you can. When you first arrive at the home, try to notice the condition of the facilities that are used for the litter. Do they appear to be clean and well kept? If you see that the whelping area is located away from the main house, ask the breeder if the puppies are ever allowed into the house and what is his or her method of socialization. Keep in mind that puppies need to be handled and socialized from birth. If they are being raised in an isolated environment and allowed human contact with only the breeder, they will have a harder time adjusting to a normal home life later on. If the breeder says that socialization is not a big con-

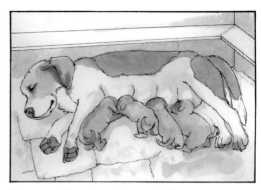

Here is a Beagle mother with her Puggle babies.

cern and you notice the puppies cowering in a corner and not responding to you, then leave.

Questions to Ask

You will want to ask the breeder many questions and see how honest he or she is with you.

1. Is the breeder aware of any indigenous health problems associated with this breed? If so, have the parents of this litter been tested for these?

2. What sort of general health problems has the breeder run across over the years? If the person has been in the business for many years and says there have never been any problems, then this could be a red flag. Dogs are living, breathing creatures with immune systems that break down from time to time and little issues are bound to arise. If the breeder is honest, he or she should have no problem letting you know about past kennel cough, parasites, and other easily treatable problems.

3. If the breeder mentions that some problems have come up from time to time, then what precautions have been taken to prevent an outbreak in the future?

The Internet can be a great way to locate a puppy.

4. Does the breeder have any references that you can follow up on?

5. How long has the person been breeding dogs in general?

6. What is the asking price of the puppy?

7. Is the price different for a male than a female? Some people selling these puppies are asking an outrageous amount for them and trying to cash in on their popularity. Also, there is no good reason to charge more for a male than for a female or vice versa. Some may charge more for smaller ones because they are less common, so that is a personal decision you will have to make.

8. Be sure to ask at what age the breeder allows the puppies to leave. You never want to take a puppy that is younger than eight weeks old. A puppy still needs to have interaction with its mother and littermates until it is at least that age. If the breeder allows the puppies to leave at six or seven weeks old, then this is not the breeder for you.

Contracts and Warranties

The best way to be sure that you are dealing with an ethical source is to make sure your purchase is done with a contract stating what the breeder offers, and what is expected of you in some cases. This is a protection for both the breeder and yourself. Many contracts will differ. Basically, they will cover health and possible congenital defects, what is and is not covered

Choosing just the right puppy may take some time.

with the purchase, and whether you can return the dog if any of these problems should arise. As a place to start, you should look for a warranty against congenital defects of at least a year. These are hereditary defects that can be life threatening. The contract will usually state specifically what defects are covered. Should your puppy contract any of these within a year, as verified in writing by a veterinarian, then the breeder will replace your puppy. The warranty may also state the things not covered, like colds, coughs, staph infections, parasites, and other common ailments that are not life threatening. This is normal, and you should not expect those things to be covered. Some breeders may include a spay or neuter clause in the contract. This is just a way to control the many accidental breedings and helps to control overpopulation. You do not have to worry about signing anything that states whether you will show the dog or not, as mixed breeds are not currently involved in shows.

Picking Out the Puppy

Do not feel pressured into buying the first puppy that you see. All puppies are cute, and you do not want to base your decision solely on looks. It is similar to choosing a mate with whom you will spend the rest of your life. Good looks are a great place to start, but there are plenty of good-looking people who would not be compatible with you. Just because a breeder claims to have show-quality dogs, champion lines, and immaculate facilities and is affiliated with all the right dog clubs does not mean the the dogs are raised well. Temperament, person-

ality, energy level, and signs of intelligence should all be factored into your decision-making process.

If you are a first-time dog owner, you may decide to let the breeder assist you in your selection. If a puppy seems to be too dominant or too submissive, you may want to consider something in between. A puppy with an extreme temperament can sometimes be difficult to raise if you have no prior experience. The breeder will have spent a lot of time with the puppies and will be better qualified to give you an idea of the temperament of each. The goal of the breeder will always be to place a puppy in the right home.

Look at the curled tail on this Puggle.

Generally speaking, you will want to choose a puppy that appears to be healthy and has no discharge coming from the eyes, nose, or ears. The puppy should be playful, happy, and outgoing. If you have a family with small children, you will want to choose a Puggle that readily approaches you, licks your hands, and wants to snuggle up to you. It will follow you around and will gently play without constantly having to use its teeth. You want the puppy to be interested in you and to want to spend a lot of time with you. This type of behavior indicates a good balance of temperament. The great thing about Puggles is that they are known to have a good temperament as a breed. Therefore you will have a better chance of having multiple choices of good puppies from the litters you may pick from. If you have the chance to look at multiple puppies, you will learn to pick out which pups are leaders, which ones are confident, which are less outgoing, which are shy, which are playful, and so on. These experiences will help you in your search so that you will know the right puppy when you meet it.

When to Get a Puppy

Never get a puppy before it is at least eight weeks old. The puppy should not be taken away from its mother earlier than this. Before eight weeks, a puppy still needs to have interaction with its mother and littermates. Some breeders will let the puppies go at five and six weeks of age to try to save some money. This is not good for the puppy, and you should not support this type of operation.

Friday is a great day to bring your new puppy home so you have the whole weekend to bond with it.

Do you have the time? You should bring home the puppy when you will be available to help it get used to its new environment. Remember that a new puppy may have trouble adjusting to new food, water, climate, sur-roundings, unfamiliar noises, and so on.

Climate concerns: Depending on your loca-tion, you may want to get your new puppy in the spring or summer. If you live in a climate that gets cold in the winter, you may have trou-ble with housebreaking because the puppy may not want to go outside. Your location is likely to have more of an impact if you had your dog shipped in from somewhere else. If you live in Florida or California, which have warm tempera-tures year-round, then getting your puppy at any time is probably going to work for you. Time of year may also not affect you if you live in an apartment and are doing potty pad or lit-ter box training. If this is the case, then you may be taking your dog outside only for exercise.

Being home: If you work and can take some vacation time, you should take a few days off to be with your new puppy. Doing this will allow you to bond with your new Puggle and help it to feel more secure now that it is away from its littermates. You should avoid bringing your new puppy home and then leaving it completely alone the very next day while you go to work. If you are not able to take off any time, try to arrange with your source to pick up your puppy on a Friday night so that you have the weekend to spend with your puppy. Being taken to a new home can be stressful for a new puppy, so it needs to be reassured by having you there.

Bad timing: There are also certain times in your life when it is best not to bring a puppy into it. Birthdays, holidays, parties, and divorces are times when too much excitement or trau-matic events may be taking place. Puppies will be aware of all the excitement and may also feel the tension being given off by various fam-ily members. This tension will add to the stress the puppy already has, and it may not feel wel-come in your home. Try to pick a time in your life that is nice and quiet, which will help make your new Puggle feel loved and welcome. Mak-ing these efforts will go a long way to ensure your new Puggle gets off to a good start.

WELCOME TO OUR HOME

Before you bring your new puppy home, you must make some preparations. With a little planning, you can make the transition for your new family member a little easier.

Its Own Space

Puggles are territorial and need a place to retreat to and think of as their own. By nature, they are den-loving animals. If given the chance, some Puggles will even dig a hollow or den to sleep in. If your Puggle does not have a place to go for naps, it may create its own den by sleeping under tables, chairs, or beds or even in laundry baskets. You should designate an area that is quiet and out of the way if possible. You may use an area in a laundry room, dining room, garage, or even a corner in your living room. If you do use a garage area, make sure the temperatures are not going to be too hot or too cold for your new puppy. This will vary greatly depending on the time of year and your location. A good rule of thumb is to make

Your new Puggle will bring much joy to your home.

sure your Puggle puppy is not exposed to temperatures above 85°F (29.4°C) or below 40°F (4.4°C) for any length of time.

The area you choose should contain a comfortable sleeping den for your Puggle. It may include a bed, playpen, crate, potty pad, or litter box in any combination you deem fit. The area should be large enough for the Puggle to sit, stand, turn around, and lie down comfortably. This will be covered in more detail later in this chapter. You want to be sure the surface area is free of toxic chemicals like lead paint, floor wax, and hazardous cleaners. You will want to remove any objects that you do not want to be chewed from your Puggle's reach. This might include electrical outlets, paper products, wood furniture, electrical wires, and chemicals. Your new puppy will likely chew and lick while exploring its new area, so you want to be sure you have created a safe environment.

Puppy Proof

Before your new Puggle comes home, you will need to examine your house thoroughly, the same way you might if you had a nine-month-old baby crawling around. Although you may not give the new puppy access to all areas of your house, it is you should guard your valuables and remove anything that may harm your Puggle. Your new Puggle will be teething. Sometimes it may prefer to go after your things versus its own toys.

Choking hazards: You will want to be sure to remove anything within the puppy's reach that is small enough to be chewed, shredded, or swallowed. Some of these things may include:

- Staples
- Pen caps
- Magazines
- Bottled water lids
- Safety pins
- Screws
- Nuts and bolts
- Nails
- Tacks
- Pencils
- Batteries
- Barbie doll accessories
- Shoes
- Jewelry
- Cell phones
- Mail

Many toxic household cleaners, fertilizers, insecticides, antifreeze, and other poisons can be fatal to an unsuspecting puppy. Because of this, you should install childproof locks on any cabinets containing these products. Under the kitchen sink is one of the most obvious locations where most people might store these items. It is also an area where you may store

=== TIP ===

Get Ready in Advance

Before you bring home your puppy, you need to:
1. Identify a designated space in the house for your new Puggle.
2. Purchase the necessary supplies.
3. Puppy proof your home.
4. Establish rules and procedures regarding the proper care of your new puppy.
5. Discuss these rules and procedures with all family members, which they should all agree to.

your garbage receptacle, which, because of a Puggle's keen sense of smell, is likely to lure your new puppy to the area.

Dangerous plants: Do not assume that your puppy is smart enough to know the difference between what is safe to chew and what is toxic

Everything is a toy in the eyes of a puppy.

These two pups are very comfortable in their new environment.

to its health. A number of household plants may be toxic to your new puppy. You should take an inventory of what plants you have and ask a professional at your local nursery if any of these may pose a threat to your Puggle. Do not assume that if the plant has not given you any health problems that it is safe for your dog. You probably have not tried to chew on any of your plants lately, but you cannot expect the same of your Puggle.

Furniture is another common item that your Puggle may be lured to chew on. Puggles will often chew on legs and corners of furniture. If you have any valuable antiques or modern furniture that may be at risk, you might want to keep them out of reach. There are some sprays that you can use on furniture to discourage

chewing. These sprays usually contain a chemical that tastes bad and will keep the dog from coming back for more. Keep in mind that some of these sprays contain alcohol and may damage the finish on your furniture, so it is wise to try them on a test area first.

Wooden blinds or plantation shutters may also be at risk. You may have a window above a couch that your Puggle wishes to look out of. If this window has blinds that are restricting the puppy's view, your puppy may attempt to chew on the wood and pull the blinds apart. Once the puppy realizes this is wood, it will probably continue to chew on the blinds. For your Puggle, this chewing of wood is similar to a puppy's desire to chew on sticks and twigs, so be aware of what is within reach.

Try to keep your puppy on the same food initially.

Essential Supplies

You must have certain supplies in your house before bringing home your new puppy. Having toys on hand is just as important as having the proper food readily available.

Food: The first essential you need to get for your new Puggle is food. You should find out what the breeder has been feeding the puppy up until now and get yourself some of that brand. Initially, you should keep your puppy on the same food and feeding schedule as the breeder. Doing this will provide your new Pug-

gle with a familiar routine amid all the new changes. If you decide you want to switch to a better-quality food after that, transition over a week. You will need to introduce gradually the new food a little bit at a time, until the old one is gone. Puggles are not generally picky eaters, so the transition to another food will usually be easier than it might be with other breeds.

Collar and leash: You will need to get a martingale nylon or cotton-webbed collar. This collar should be adjustable from 7–10 inches (18–25 cm) as it will be used for the first couple of months. If it is properly fit, it will be tight enough not to slip over the head and loose enough to allow an adult finger to slip under it. You should never put a choke chain or other adult training collar on a puppy.

In addition to the collar, you will need to get a strong leash. This leash should be 4–6 feet (120–180 cm) long and preferably made out of the same materials listed for the collar. These materials are inexpensive and work great for a first collar. Down the road, you may want to consider getting a harness when your Puggle is old enough to go on walks in public.

Bowls: Dog bowls come in a variety of shapes, sizes, and materials. You will want to get a bowl that is not easily tipped over. Puggles like to play and may attempt to chew on a new bowl you have placed into their area. Some hard plastic and stainless steel bowls are made with rubber bottoms. The rubber is used so that the bowl remains stationary and does not slide around. You should get separate water and food bowls. If you get the type that has two bowls in one, you may have to change the water every time you change the food. Another effective anti-tip water bowl is the type that hangs from a crate or playpen. It will have hooks or clasps that are easily screwed into place. Some puppies are picky about the material their bowl is made of, so you may have to try out a few.

Puppy bed: There are a few things to consider when purchasing a dog bed. You should usually wait until your Puggle is potty trained before getting a more permanent bed. Your puppy will be prone to accidents early on, and you do not want it to get used to soiling its bed. Even if you wash the bed often, a small trace of urine smell may linger and convince your puppy going potty where it sleeps is all right. When it is old

These puppies enjoy chewing toys on their bed.

enough, you will want to see what position your Puggle likes to sleep in before getting a new bed. If your dog likes to stretch out, you should probably go with a traditional square or rectangular-shaped bed. If your pet likes to sleep curled up, then a donut-shaped cuddler bed may be preferable. In this type, your Puggle will sleep in the center and be surrounded by a circle of cushioned comfort. In either case, you will want to make sure that the bed is strong and made of a durable material like canvas. Puggles generally like to chew, so you want to avoid the foam beds that have a thin material around them. Your Puggle can easily shred one of these into quite a mess in a short period of time and can also swallow the little foam pieces.

Toys: Toys are important to have around right from the beginning. Your Puggle will need a few different chew toys to choose from. You will need to buy a variety of types until you can

It's bath time for these puppies.

identify something that your Puggle really likes. A good place to start is the hard rubber toys that are shaped like bones. Edible pork skin chews are well received by Puggles. These come in a variety of shapes and sizes. There are also rubber toys that have little bells inside that make noise. Rope toys are a good bet and may satisfy your Puggle's need to tug at something. There are hollow rubber toys that you can stuff with treats that your Puggle will probably really go for. Some Puggles may even like the canvas toys that you freeze first.

Whatever toy you choose, you want to make sure it is not something that will fall apart into little pieces or has stuffing that can come out. Puggles are very active chewers. Only the hardest and strongest chews and toys should be offered to them. You want to avoid rawhide, soft plastic, and real bones as well. If you have a suspicion that one of the toys you have may not be safe, make sure your Puggle is supervised when playing with it. Better still, just throw it out. Your Puggle's safety, not your wallet, should be your priority.

Grooming supplies: You will want to be sure and have a brush and comb handy for your new Puggle. A good hound brush will be the best type for your dog's coat. Although a Puggle's coat is not very long, brushing regularly will assist with a shedding dog and make the coat look its best. The comb can be used periodically to check for fleas and any other type of skin irritation that may be present. You may want to consider getting a set of nail clippers for your puppy. Some people prefer to have their dog's nails trimmed at the veterinarian. If you chose to clip the nails yourself, be careful not to clip them too short and risk injuring the pink area called the quick. If you should happen to cut into the quick, it will bleed. You may need to use some styptic powder to stop the bleeding.

Crates and Playpens

If you are unfamiliar with the use of crates in dog training, their use may seem to be a form of punishment, but this is not the case. As humans, we tend to lock up our prisoners in a confined cell, as a form of punishment, so it is understandable to have reservations about locking your dog in a crate. The truth is that crates are not cruel. They actually provide your dog with a safe place to call its own. Having this crate will provide your Puggle with a sense of security and facilitate the housebreaking process. Although it is not advisable to lock your puppy in its crate all day, allowing it to sleep in its crate will aid in the puppy getting used to being in the crate should you need to transport it. Your puppy will seek out the comfort and retreat of a den, and you just happen to be providing your Puggle with a fancier one than it could have found itself.

You will want to purchase a crate that is close to 24 inches (60 cm) long by 18 inches (45 cm) wide by 21 inches (53 cm) high. It should be made out of wire or fiberglass and be well ventilated all the way around. As a permanent crate, try to stay away from the collapsible type as these are best used for traveling. Be sure to place a comfortable bed or blanket inside the crate for your puppy. More than likely, the pet store where you bought your crate will have many beds to choose from that are designed for crates.

Crate training is the most popular and preferred method of housebreaking used by breeders and trainers. The common theory behind crate training is that dogs instinctively will not usually soil in their den area. By nature, your Puggle desires to be clean and would prefer waiting to relieve itself until you release it from its crate. The crate is not a place to put your dog when it is in trouble nor is it a place to put your puppy when playtime with you is over.

While crate training, you should put the crate into an area that is out of the way and not subject to heavy traffic. There will be many

Placing a playpen around your puppy's new crate will provide a controlled environment.

times throughout the day when your puppy will be sleeping and would prefer not to be disturbed. If you place your Puggle into the crate as it is falling asleep, your puppy will come to know this area as its bed. Similarly, if you place your puppy into the area where you would like it to go potty as it is waking up, this area will eventually become the spot where your dog relieves itself. We will cover crate training and housebreaking in much more detail in the training chapter of this book.

You should use a playpen to surround the puppy's crate. You will want to get a playpen that is 4 feet (120 cm) by 4 feet (120 cm) and at least 30 inches (76 cm) high. This will give your puppy an area to play in when it is not sleeping. A playpen is the perfect solution for when you must be away from your Puggle for any length of time. This will allow your puppy to relieve itself in one area, sleep in another, and play with its toys in yet another. Your new Puggle will naturally want to explore every area of your house if you let it. For this reason, it is best to confine your Puggle's play space to the playpen when you are

Be as comforting and affectionate as you can in the early stages.

not present. This will also help you establish which areas of your home are off-limits.

Having a playpen will also confine potty accidents to one location and help protect carpets and wood floors. A common practice is to place a heavy-gauge vinyl plastic sheet underneath the playpen area to protect your floors further. By using the vinyl, you will better protect your floors from permanent damage and make cleaning up a snap for you. Tape down the vinyl to the floor on all sides. Do not be surprised if your Puggle attempts to tug at the vinyl or make holes in it. Try to avoid having a taped seam within the perimeter of the playpen. Also, be sure to have something available that your Puggle likes to chew on at all times. This will help to prevent your puppy from chewing a hole in the vinyl floor.

Arriving Home

Now that you have your supplies, have done your puppy proofing, and have picked out a spot for your new family member, it is time to bring your Puggle home. When you first get home, allow your Puggle to walk around outside of your home for a bit before entering. Although everyone in the house may be excited about the new Puggle, it is best to make the initial introduction low-key so you do not overwhelm the puppy. This will likely be the first time it has been separated from its littermates and mother. Human contact is important at this stage for reassurance, but you have to tread lightly.

First, you want to place your new Puggle into the area you have designated. Next, allow it to sniff around and explore this new area. Then, each person should gradually spend some time with the pup, one at a time. You will want to crouch down to the puppy's level and allow it to sniff your hands while you gently pet it. Remember that for your puppy, there are many new noises, smells, and people, plus a new location. For this reason, you will want to be as affectionate and comforting as you are able in these early stages. This will also help in forming an immediate bond with your new puppy.

Let the Puggle decide: Your new Puggle may want to play but will probably tire quickly. Remember that your puppy may have experienced a long airplane ride or an extended period of time in the car. These will have been firsts for your puppy, and the stress may have taken its toll. For this reason, you should let the

We are ready to take a nap.

puppy decide what it wants to do first instead of trying to set some kind of schedule. After about an hour, you can try to give your new puppy something to eat or drink. You should be available to play if it wants to play. If it wants to sleep, then allow it to sleep.

Go slowly: Allow at least a day to go by before allowing any friends or neighbors to come by and meet your new addition. Your Puggle needs time to get used to the immediate family members who live in the house. Do not overwhelm your puppy with too many unfamiliar faces or experiences all at once. You should also keep your household as quiet as possible for the first day to allow the puppy time to explore and adjust to its new environment.

The first night: Now that your new Puggle has explored its new area, met the family, eaten its first meal, and relieved itself, it is time for bed. You need to keep in mind that this is your puppy's first night alone in an unfamiliar place. It is important to keep the new area as warm

and comfortable as possible. You can expect to hear some whining at various times throughout the night. This is your puppy's attempt to let others know where it is in the hopes of drawing some company its way. When your Puggle starts to whine, you need to ignore it and be strong. Unless you want to set a precedent of playing at various times throughout the night, you must resist the temptation. Your puppy will be fine and will eventually fall asleep.

One comforting thing you can do is to place a piece of bedding from its former home that may have the scent of its littermates on it into its new bed. You can also try putting a ticking clock next to the puppy in the hopes of simulating another beating heart nearby. Pet stores also sell little gadgets that actually have the sound of a beating heart. Some experts advise putting a hot water bottle into your puppy's bed for added warmth. Be patient. You may have to try a few different methods to curb the whining, but it will not last forever.

Veterinary medicine has become far more sophisticated and complex in recent years. If a veterinarian uses the best technology together with the latest breakthroughs, we can expect our pets to live longer and healthier lives.

How to Find a Veterinarian

Finding a good veterinarian should not be a difficult task. You should ask your friends and coworkers who own dogs how they feel about their veterinarian. Feel free to contact other animal professionals like dog trainers, groomers, and local pet stores to get their opinion. Your selection process should not be based on only personality and competence but also upon location and distance from your house. You are going to want your veterinarian to be close by in case you have an emergency or need to make several visits for treatment. You will want to find a clinic that has hours that will accommodate your schedule and find out if they provide 24-hour emergency coverage. If they refer their patients' after-hours emergencies somewhere else, then find out where it is located so you are not caught off guard in the event of an emergency.

Interview the clinic: You should visit all the nearby veterinary clinics in your area and explain to them that you are getting a new dog. Ask if you might have a look around the facilities and meet at least one of the doctors. Find out how much they charge for a general office visit, nail clipping, tooth cleaning, spaying or neutering, and so on. Do not be afraid to inquire about these costs with the veterinarian. Compare the costs at each of the clinics you visit. Sophisticated veterinary services can be very costly these days, and many important decisions are based on financial considerations.

Different veterinarians: All of the veterinarians that you will encounter are licensed and should have their certificates and diplomas clearly displayed in their waiting rooms. Most veterinarians can perform routine surgeries like spaying, neutering, sewing up wounds, and

Good health and temperament are desirable traits to look for in a Puggle.

docking tails. When a problem arises that is beyond the scope of your veterinarian's expertise, you will be referred to a specialist. These are doctors that have undergone additional studies and internships:

- Veterinary cardiologists treat heart problems.
- Veterinary dentists specialize in tooth and gum problems.
- Veterinary dermatologists focus on skin problems.
- Veterinary ophthalmologists treat eye problems.
- Veterinary radiologists work with X-rays.

When you do finally pick a veterinarian that you are happy with, make sure you establish a good rapport early on. You and your veterinarian will be working as an ongoing team for the well being of your Puggle's health. Your veterinarian should consider your observations and concerns and then clearly explain to you what is going on with your Puggle.

Be sure to schedule your veterinarian appointment as soon as possible.

The First Veterinarian Visit

You should bring your new Puggle for its first checkup within 48 to 72 hours after you get it. A puppy/dog may appear to be healthy on the outside and still have a serious problem that is not evident to the average person. The majority of dogs have some type of minor flaw that will never cause a serious problem. However, if it turns out to be serious, you will want to consider the potential consequences as early as possible. You will need to decide whether to keep the dog or not, to form attachments that may need to be broken, to consider potential long-term costs, and so on. One thing to keep in mind is that most reputable breeders will usually have some type of return policy or guarantee on their litters.

When you arrive at the veterinary clinic, try to keep your Puggle on your lap or in a small crate. Do not let it play with, bark at, or scare

TIP

Provide Regular Attention

Even the best veterinarian, strongest body, and best genetic background will not allow a dog to live a healthy life if it does not receive regular attention from its owner. Dogs are at risk of getting infections and parasites. However, they are also at risk from natural hazards and accidents. It is your responsibility to take preventive measures to ensure your dog's health.

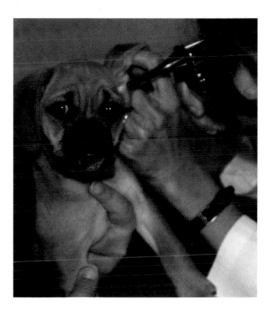

This Puggle is doing well at his first veterinary visit.

any of the other animals who may be sick. If you believe that your dog may have a potentially contagious illness, be sure to let the clinic know ahead of time in case they want you to use an alternate entrance. When they call you into the exam room, let your veterinarian know if there is a chance that your dog may bite. Veterinarians are always appreciative if you give them a heads up on any potential outburst that your dog may have when being handled. They prefer a dog that is clean and under control during the examination.

The checkup: The veterinarian is going to check your Puggle's overall health condition, which may include the following:

✔ Checking the respiration
✔ Feeling the abdomen, muscles, and joints
✔ Listening to the heart
✔ Checking the condition of the skin and coat
✔ Examining the eyes
✔ Checking the ears
✔ Checking the mouth, gums, and teeth

The veterinarian will probably ask you about your pet's eating and elimination schedule and invite you to present any questions or concerns that you may have. You should always prepare and write down any questions you have before you come. You will be exposed to a lot of new information you were not expecting, and it is easy to forget to ask your veterinarian what you wanted to know. The veterinarian will discuss the proper diet and amounts that you are giving your Puggle. If this is different from what your breeder recommended, then let the veterinarian know and get his or her opinion.

An Ounce of Prevention

Practicing preventive measures is always going to be easier and cheaper in the long run than battling illnesses and diseases. If you have the chance to get your Puggle from a properly bred litter, do it. You want to be sure the parents were selected based on their genetic disease profiles. The mother should have been properly vaccinated and free of all parasites, both internal and external. A healthy dam is able to pass on some disease resistance to her puppies lasting about eight to ten weeks after birth. On the other hand, an unhealthy mother can also pass on infections and parasites. This is why it is important to try to get as healthy a puppy as you can.

All puppies should be weaned from the mother by about the eighth week. A puppy will be able to adapt to people and other dogs more easily if it remains with its mother for at least

Make a Balanced Decision

When choosing a veterinary clinic, try not to make your decision based solely on cost. Using the least-expensive clinic may short-change both your pet and your pocketbook in the long run if the veterinarian makes improper diagnoses or prescribes ineffective treatments.

eight weeks. After that point, you need to maintain your Puggle's health with immunizations and spaying/neutering.

Immunizations

All dogs require yearly vaccinations to help protect them from the most common life-threatening diseases. Medically speaking, these vaccines are your dog's best preventive measure. The idea is to immunize your dog before your dog ever has a chance to be exposed to or contract any of the diseases. For this reason, it is critical that you keep up with your dog's vaccinations. Whatever the age of your dog, you should bring the vaccination records with you on your first visit. If you have a puppy, the breeder should have taken care of the initial vaccinations up until the time that you took possession of the animal. Most veterinarians will differ slightly in the way they handle vaccinations.

Most veterinarians will begin the puppy immunization process from the age of 5–6 weeks. Usually this will be a series of combined injections given every 2–3 weeks. This series of injections is typically given through at least 12–14 weeks and is called the DHLPP. The DHLPP is designed to immunize your dog against parvovirus, distemper, hepatitis, leptospirosis, and parainfluenza. It is not uncommon for your dog to receive an additional parvovirus vaccine at 16–18 weeks of age. The vaccination for rabies is usually given between 3–6 months, depending on your location. A kennel cough (bordetella) vaccination is recommended and can be given anytime beyond the age of 6 weeks. It is generally accepted that the maternal distemper antibodies are gone by week 12. However, it is generally not known when all of a puppy's maternal antibodies are no longer present. For this reason, immunizations are started at such an early age.

Neutering/Spaying

The next thing to consider is whether or not to spay or neuter your new puppy. Unless you are going to be breeding or showing your dog, this procedure should be performed at about the six-month mark. Most veterinarians are going to advise having it done, as there are many benefits. Besides eliminating the possibility of unwanted pregnancies, it inhibits breast and ovarian cancer in females and prostate cancer in males. It is quite rare to find a bitch diagnosed with breast cancer that was spayed before her first heat. An older female who is unspayed may also develop a life-threatening disease called pyometra (an infected uterus).

Spaying is done while the female is under a general anesthetic and is much easier on a young dog. The surgery removes the ovaries and the uterus. It is important for the doctor to remove all of the ovarian tissue. If there is any left behind, the female might still be attracted to males. Neutering the male involves removing the testicles but leaving the scrotum. Neutering

A healthy dog is a happy one. Many diseases can now be prevented with proper vaccinations.

the male at an early age will help prevent some unwanted male behaviors like hormonal aggressiveness. Also, many neutered males will never hike their legs up and mark their territory.

Diseases

Many serious and life-threatening diseases that were once common in dogs can now be prevented with vaccines. In many areas, vaccinations against these diseases are legally required—especially against rabies. Check with your veterinarian for the schedule of mandatory vaccines.

Distemper: This disease is virtually incurable if contracted. This is caused by a virus that will attack every tissue in the dog's body. The symptoms are similar to a common cold in a human being. The Puggle can have a runny nose and watery eyes that may be followed by a thick yellow discharge within a few days. This is usually followed by a fever and gastrointestinal problems like poor appetite, vomiting, and diarrhea. Seizures will occur in the later stages and finally death. This is still a common disease, with puppies and senior dogs being the most at risk.

Hepatitis: This is a highly contagious virus that is most serious in young puppies. The virus is spread by coming in contact with an infected animal or its stool and urine. The virus will attack the liver and kidneys. The symptoms can be high fever, depression, lack of appetite, bloody stools, and vomiting. If an animal does recover, it may be afflicted with chronic illnesses.

Leptospirosis: This disease is transmitted by coming in contact with the urine of an infected dog, mouse, or other wild animal. Your dog can also become infected by swimming in or drinking infected water. The symptoms are severe fever, abdominal pain, depression, internal bleeding, and jaundice. This disease was fatal before the vaccine was developed. It is no longer a common disease but can still be transmitted to humans if present.

Parvovirus: This is a highly contagious disease that was first noted in the late 1970s and is still fatal. However, this disease can be manageable with proper vaccinations, early diagnosis, and prompt treatment. It attacks the bone marrow and intestinal tract. Symptoms include depression, loss of appetite, vomiting, diarrhea, and collapse. There will be very little urine output if any, and the nose, mouth, and eyes will become dry. Immediate medical attention is needed if there is any chance of survival.

Rabies: This disease is transmitted by the saliva and carried by a variety of varmints, including foxes, skunks, bats, raccoons, and wild cats. Rabies attacks nerve tissue and causes the brain to become inflamed. This inflammation will cause erratic behavior and neurological problems. Symptoms include paralysis, withdrawal, unusual erratic behavior, and finally death. Rabies is endemic and can easily be spread to humans. If you happen to see a mammal of any kind acting strangely, call your local animal control specialist. If your pet happens to get bitten by a wild animal of any kind, you should immediately get it to the veterinarian to treat the wound and get a test for rabies. The disease is starting to reappear in suburban areas.

Bordetella (kennel cough): The symptoms of this bacterial infection are coughing, sneezing, hacking, and retching. This is usually accompanied by a nasal discharge that can last up to several weeks. The current vaccines available do not entirely protect against the disease because there are many strains. This disease is highly contagious. Your veterinarian may require you to use an alternate entrance to the clinic if he or she suspects your dog might be infected. This infection is not usually fatal but can advance into a serious bronchopneumonia.

Coronavirus: This disease was first noted in the late 1970s about a year before parvovirus. It is often misdiagnosed as parvovirus because of the similar symptoms associated with it. This virus is also very contagious but not life threatening. Symptoms include a foul-smelling yellow-brown stool or diarrhea. There may also be depression, dehydration, and vomiting.

Lyme disease: This disease was first seen in 1976 by people who lived in Lyme, Connecticut. These people lived in close proximity to the deer tick that transmits the disease. These ticks are difficult to spot because they are about the size of a pinhead. Symptoms may include fever, acute lameness, loss of appetite, and swelling of the joints. These are usually accompanied by a painless red rash. If the disease is treated early, it is possible to cure the dog completely.

Your veterinarian can let you know if you live in an endemic area. If you suspect that you live in an infected area, you should talk to your veterinarian and take the appropriate precautions before you go for a hike or a walk with your dog.

External Parasites

External parasites are not just an annoyance. They can carry dangerous pathogens. In addition, external parasites can leave a dog and bite

Your dog will spend a fair amount of time outdoors, so you need to take precautions for fleas.

humans. Therefore, prevention and quick treatment of infestations are essential.

Fleas: Of all the problems to which dogs are prone, these little pests are the most well-known and most frustrating to deal with. Although prevention of a flea infestation is relatively inexpensive compared with treatment, it is a difficult task to achieve in some cases. Besides carrying diseases and parasites, fleas can make the daily routine of a dog quite miserable. Some Puggles are allergic to even a couple of fleas on their bodies. In many cases, it takes only a single bite to get an allergic reaction. The main cause is a protein found in the flea's saliva. The dog then begins to scratch, chew, and destroy its skin and coat because of the fleas. This usually results in a reddening of the area and the formation of

a hot spot. This type of reaction is generally going to require a trip to the veterinarian for treatment.

If you do have a flea infestation, no single product is likely to fix the problem. It will need to be combated on several fronts. Not only is the dog going to need treatment but so will its entire living environment. Dogs carry fleas inside with them. The fleas then lay their eggs in the carpeting, on furniture, and anywhere your dog happens to travel in the house. Many products are available that will kill both the larvae and adult fleas. For the house and yard, there are plenty of flea sprays and flea bombs that you can purchase. Keep in mind that these sprays are generally only effective for one to two weeks.

For your dog, flea collars are not generally very effective. At most, they will keep fleas away from your dog's neck and head for a period of time. The other problem is that many dog owners tend to leave the collar on the dog long after the effects of the collar have worn off.

Flea dips following your dog's bath tend to be the cheapest way to go, but they can be a messy experience to administer. These will also last about one to two weeks. The disadvantage of sprays and dips is that some dogs may have an allergic reaction to the chemicals. You can find some effective shampoos and medical treatments through your veterinarian and some pet shops.

An oral tablet came onto the market around 1995. This treatment decreases the flea population by sterilizing the female flea but will not kill adult fleas. If your dog is one who suffers from a flea bite allergy, then it will still be at risk with this treatment.

The most popular treatment in recent years is probably permethrin. This is applied to the back of the dog in one or two places once a month. The chemical makes its way around the dog's coat and also gets deposited in the areas that the dog frequents. This product works as a repellent and causes the fleas to get hot feet and jump off the affected areas.

It is important to note that some of the products are not suitable for young puppies and can be hazardous to their health. Check with your veterinarian before using products on your puppy.

Thankfully, many safe and effective flea products are on the market today. Fleas are becoming less and less of a problem. Prevention is still your best bet though, so be sure to consult with your veterinarian as soon as possible to learn about your options.

Ticks: Although not as common as fleas, ticks can be found in many different places of the world. They tend to live in the same areas where fleas are found. They also like to hide in cracks and in the seams of walls. Unlike fleas, ticks do not bite. They dig their probe into the skin of the dog and drink the blood. The jaws of a tick can carry various diseases such as Lyme disease and Rocky Mountain spotted fever. They can also cause tick paralysis.

While examining your dog for ticks that may have lodged themselves into the skin, be sure to check around the ears, armpits, and genital areas. If you do happen to find one, try to smear it with petroleum jelly. This will suffocate the tick, and it will proceed to back out of the skin. If you find that it does not want to back out, then you can grab it with a pair of tweezers and gently twist while pulling it out. Try not to tug on the tick, as its head may remain lodged in the skin and cause an abscess or infection that requires veterinary treatment. If you suspect ticks in your area, there is a collar you can get that does a great job. The ticks do not like the collar and will back out of the skin of a dog that wears one. Otherwise, the treatment will be the same as for fleas.

Two adult Puggles spend time with their Boston Terrier buddy.

Sarcoptic mange: This is actually caused by a mite that is difficult to find on the skin. Just like fleas, these mites can cause a great deal of itching. The *Sarcoptes* mites are highly contagious to other dogs and to humans. These mites do not live very long on humans, though. They are microscopic in size and will try to take up permanent residency on your dog. The cycle of this mite lasts up to three weeks. The mites tend to live in the top layer of a dog's skin and will gravitate to areas with the least amount of hair. The word mange is another term used for infestation.

Demodectic mange: This is caused by the *Demodex* mite. Unlike the *Sarcoptes* mite, this mite is not contagious or transferred from one dog to another. This type of mange is passed from the dam to her puppies. It affects the puppies between three to ten months of age. These mites live in the dog's hair follicles and sebaceous glands in very large numbers. You may start to see areas of balding around the eyes, lips, and forelegs of your dog. There is not much itching with this mite unless there is a secondary infection. Most dogs will recover

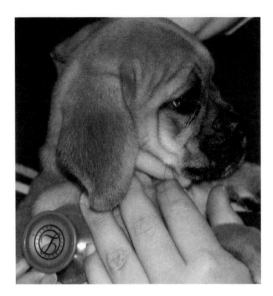

without any treatment though topical treatments are available through your veterinarian.

Cheyletiellosis: This is caused by a hook-mouthed mite called the *Cheyletiella*. Another term used for this condition is walking dandruff. This mite causes intense itching and lives on the surface of the dog's skin. It can be found in dogs, cats, rabbits, and humans. You may find yellow-gray scales on the back, rump, and top of the head and nose. This mite is easily transferred to other animals through direct and indirect contact. The dandruff may or may not be itchy depending on your dog's reaction. If left untreated, this mite could infect an entire kennel.

Otodectic mange: This problem is caused by *Otodectes cynotis*, also known as the ear mite. This condition is mostly found in the outer ear canal of the dog. Symptoms can include a shaking of the head and scratching of the ears. Your veterinarian will be looking for some darkened brown discharge in the outer ear area. Treatment will include a flushing of the ears to kill

any eggs that may be present. It is not uncommon for treatment to last up to a month.

Internal Parasites

As the exterior part of the dog's body will be host to fleas, ticks, and mites, the inside also is inhabited by a variety of parasites. The majority of these parasites are in the worm family. Most animals, including birds, fish, dogs, cats, and even humans, have parasites and worms that live inside their bodies. A worm infection is relatively easy to control if treated. If left untreated, though, you may start to see other medical problems begin to occur in the dog's weakened state.

Roundworm: This is a spaghetti-like worm also known as *Toxocara canis*. Puppies can get this while in the mother's uterus and also through lactation. Adult dogs acquire this by eating contaminated feces or killing an infected rodent. Hundreds of thousands of roundworm eggs can be in 1 ounce (28 g) of infected dog feces. In puppies, these roundworms cause a bloated or potbellied appearance, coughing, diarrhea, and vomiting. Although this infection can kill a puppy, adult dogs are not generally at risk of death. They can, however, have severe problems as the roundworm larvae travel through the bloodstream to the lungs and trachea. There is also a danger of humans getting infected as well. Keeping your dog and its disposal areas clean is the best preventive measure for roundworms.

Hookworm: This is a microscopic intestinal worm that can be dangerous in dogs and cats as well as humans. This worm can create an iron deficiency that can lead to severe anemia. The worm will use its teeth to attach itself to the dog's intestines and moves from place to place about six times a day. As the worm relocates itself, the dog will lose blood and can become anemic. The symptoms can include anemia, weight loss, dark-colored stools, a pale coloration, and general fatigue. Although puppies can be born with the worms, humans can contract them through the skin.

Hookworms are relatively easy to get rid of with a number of effective medications available from your veterinarian. As a preventive measure, be sure to use a pooper-scooper or disposable gloves when handling your dog's feces. Also, try to keep your children from playing in areas where dogs and cats may have defecated.

Whipworm: Here in the United States, the whipworm is the most commonly found parasitic worm in dogs. The technical name for this is *Trichuris vulpis*. These worms will attach themselves to the lower end of the dog's intestines, where they will feed. Some of the symptoms are upset stomach, diarrhea, and colic. These worms are quite possibly the hardest to get rid of when diagnosed. The reason for this is their extended life cycle.

The eggs of these worms can last for months or years undetected in the dog's body. They can remain dormant until the ideal conditions allow them to mature. When this happens, they spend their larval stage in the small intestine, their adult stage in the large intestine, and finally pass their infected eggs into the dog's feces. The only known way to detect whipworms is through examining the feces, which are seldom found. Because of the unusual nature of their life cycle, the whipworm is

Preventive maintenance is important for your Puggle's health.

difficult to treat. Their eggs are resistant to many environmental factors and can reinfect your dog if it comes into contact with infected eggs on the ground. The best line of defense against this tricky parasite is prevention. Having a fenced yard to keep out unwanted stray dogs is helpful, as well as always using a pooper-scooper for cleanup.

Tapeworms: These come in many different species and are all carried by fleas. The tapeworm that is most common to dogs is called *Dipylidium caninum*. These are generally seen as ricelike segments located near your dog's anus. They are long and flat and can be up to several feet long. Your dog will ingest the flea by lick-

Notice the similarities between this Puggle and the Beagle next to it.

ing and chewing, and this starts the tapeworm cycle. Your dog can also ingest these tapeworms by consuming any portion of an infected rodent, rabbit, or large game animal. Humans are also at risk of getting infected with tapeworms. Tapeworms are not life threatening for dogs, but they can cause severe liver damage in humans. Because of their small size, it is not difficult to have one passed to your hand. So be careful when handling fleas.

Heartworm: This is a thin worm that lives in the dog's heart and surrounding blood vessels of the heart. These worms can be up to 12 inches (30 cm) long and be up to 200 in number. Some of the symptoms may include loss of appetite, loss of energy, coughing, anemia, and the formation of a pot belly. The worm is spread by mosquitoes. The mosquito will first drink the blood of an infected dog that carries the larvae. The larvae will then develop inside the mosquito that will then pass them on to the next dog it bites. Although it is a life-threatening disease, it is not easily contracted by your dog. It is expensive to treat should your dog become infected, but prevention is easily attained through various available products.

Consult with your veterinarian about which is the best course to take.

Puggle Health Risks

There is much speculation in the dog world about whether a hybrid will have less health risks than a purebred dog. Most experts agree that purebred dogs tend to have a higher incidence of hereditary genetic defects. This is because the majority of purebred breeders are focused on physical and temperament traits in the hopes of producing a dog that will show well. The best purebred breeders will do their best to reduce these risks but cannot guarantee them. These conditions can be painful for both owner and dog, as well as very costly.

Wallace Havens, recognized hybrid breeder and creator of the Puggle, not only agrees that his hybrids have less health problems, but he gives a five-year guarantee on any health defects from Puggles that he has bred. This is virtually unheard of in the dog world today. That is what you call putting your money where your mouth is. Like any dog, the Puggle can be at risk for a host of known diseases and illnesses. Because the Puggle is a cross between a purebred Pug and a purebred Beagle, we will cover the most common diseases found in these two lines. These will be the ones for which the Puggle is most at risk of getting.

Mange (Pug): Mange comes in two basic forms: sarcoptic and demodectic. Sarcoptic mange is a much more serious problem to deal with, but it is very unusual to find in a Pug. You can find out more about this mange in the section "External Parasites."

Pugs are more likely to get demodectic mange. If contracted, it will generally occur between the

Most experts agree that mixed breed dogs are less likely to contract congenital health problems than their purebred counterparts.

ages of four and ten months. Mange is a term used for an infestation of mites. It is generally found on most dogs but normally kept at bay by the dog's own immune system. If the dog experiences a traumatic event such as cutting teeth, being left alone for extended periods of time, or taking an airplane ride at a young age, its immune system can become weakened and therefore become more susceptible to getting mange. You may start to see areas of balding around the eyes, lips, and forelegs of your dog. If this is left untreated, it will be followed by skin irritations and secondary bacterial infections. This is very painful for your dog and will cause it to scratch incessantly. If caught early, the effects will be minimal. The good thing is that once your dog has had demodectic mange, it will seldom return.

Entropion (Pug): Another common problem found in Pugs is a condition called entropion. This is a condition where the eyelashes rub directly against the surface of the eye. If this is not treated, it can lead to blindness. This is a common problem found in all flat-nosed canine breeds because of their short muzzle. This may be lessened in the Puggle because the muzzle is longer than in a Pug. Some symptoms of entropion include excess tear production, squinting, and staining of the hair right below the eyes. Early detection is a key factor, as it is with most illnesses. This condition is easily corrected by a minor surgery performed by your veterinarian.

Patellar luxation (Pug): This is a condition that affects the kneecap of a dog. This condition is also known as a trick knee. This condition occurs when the upper leg bone (femur) slips out of place and does not make normal contact with the lower leg bone (stifle). Although this condition is not as common in Pugs as it is in larger breeds, this has been turning up more often in Pugs in recent years. Patellar luxation can start off as a once in a while condition and turn into a permanent one. A fairly simple corrective surgery is available. As always, consult with your veterinarian about your options if you suspect this condition.

Pug dog encephalitis: This disease is found only in Pugs. It is a breed-specific disease. Other dog breeds can get general encephalitis, but the nature of this particular disease is unique to Pugs. Encephalitis in medical terms means a swelling of the brain. The unique quality of this strain is that it inflames the brain as well as its outer membrane. Some causes that have been identified are bacteria, viruses, fungi, and other organisms. There appear to be some additional causes that are not known.

Some of the symptoms will include circling, seizures, pressing the head against an object, faulty eyesight, and weakness on one or both sides of the body. These symptoms can become increasingly worse as the condition gains momentum. Although most tests will come back normal, a rise in the white blood cell count of the spinal fluid has been noted. A temporary relief of symptoms may be helpful by using prednisone. However, there are no known cases of survival once the disease has been identified. Because this is a fairly new disease, it is recommended that you have your veterinarian contact a veterinary college to seek guidance on treatment should your dog become infected.

Epilepsy (Beagle): This disease comes in two general degrees of severity. The first is called the petit mal. The symptoms may appear as the dog simply spacing out for a few minutes. The dog will then act subdued or disoriented for a few moments. This is followed by the dog acting as if nothing ever happened. The next degree is called a grand mal. The symptoms can be a stiffening of the entire body, loss of muscular control, and convulsions. The convulsion can last for several minutes and may appear as though your dog is about to die. This too is followed by a brief disorientation, and then the dog acts like nothing ever happened. The milder form presents no real problem for the dog. However, grand mal fits will usually require medication. Never breed an epileptic dog.

Cherry eye (Beagle): This is an infection and swelling of the third eyelid. This condition is quite common in Beagles and can be treated with a relatively simple procedure. At first glance, this condition appears to look worse than it really is. Although the swelling and redness are quite obvious to us, many dogs do not seem to notice that

Preventative maintenance is important for your Puggle's health.

there is even a problem. Recurrence of a cherry eye is not uncommon. If a cherry eye recurs, let your veterinarian know. A secondary surgery will often be required and be performed by your veterinarian or an ophthalmology specialist.

Lameness (Beagle): This is a condition where the dog carries one foot off the ground. If your dog has been running around outside or in a field somewhere, the cause may be as simple as a thorn in the foot. This may be something you can feel around for and remove yourself without much fuss. A minor cut will not usually have the need for any treatment. If the foot appears to have any swelling or redness associated with it, then your dog may have another condition and require antibiotics. If you cannot find anything on the foot, your dog may have a bruised or twisted knee or some other joint used for walking. Beagles do not appear to be bothered much when they have to carry one foot off the ground. It is important to note that

Lyme disease, disk problems, and kidney disease start out with similar symptoms. If the condition continues for an extended time, you should seek medical attention for your dog.

A Puggle Breeder's Perspective

Wallace Havens has been breeding dogs, both hybrid and purebreds, for over 35 years. He currently has two veterinarians working full-time at his facility in Wisconsin. Wallace is the recognized creator of the Puggle as we know it. He was the first to coin the term and to breed the mix regularly. He has bred and sold literally thousands of Puggles as of this writing and is considered to be the foremost expert. According to Wallace and his veterinarians, of all the diseases listed here regarding Pugs and Beagles, the only one he has seen is cherry eye. It occurs only in about 1 percent of Puggles. The only other thing he has seen in Puggles are mild cases of hernias.

Curious puppies and dogs tend to wander off and look for things to get into. This is not a bout of bad behavior or an attempt on their part to get a rise out of you. They get into trouble because they want to investigate the world around them. More accidents, harmful plants, and dangerous substances kill or harm dogs each year than you might think. Take a moment to think before you allow your Puggle to begin an activity. Try to be mindful of the many things that may go wrong. It is up to you to protect your dog from harmful substances and potentially hazardous situations. Some of the following suggestions may seem like common sense, but they are certainly worth mentioning.

Playing Without a Leash

You do not want to allow your new dog to be playing off the leash anywhere near major streets or in high traffic areas unless there is an enclosed fence. If the area is fenced, you will still want to keep the dog on a leash until you have walked the perimeter of the fence and checked for any openings that your dog may escape through. If there is a hole somewhere, you can be sure your Puggle will find it as it explores. Do not count on your dog's obedience to prevent it from wandering into a hazardous area. If you live near the woods and allow your dog to roam freely, be on the lookout for leg traps that may have been placed by hunters or poachers. You should also carry a first aid kit with you in the event of cuts, scrapes, bee stings, snake bites, and so on. It takes only one accident to harm or end your pet's life, so be careful.

Swimming

If you want to allow your dog to go swimming, then be sure that the water area is a safe place. If it is a moving body of water, then you must consider the current both on and below the surface. Even though your Puggle is part Beagle, and is considered to be a good swimmer, it could be swept away with a mild undercurrent. If you live in the southern states near marshes and swamps, then you have to be wary of alligators and crocodiles that may be lurking in shallow water. Your new puppy will not have any idea of the danger this poses and is likely to wander toward the reptile. Another concern is any toxic substances that may be present in the water, as all dogs tend to drink some amount of water as they swim.

Be sure to keep pesticides out of the reach of your curious puppy.

HAZARDS

Toxic Plants

Toxic plants come in many varieties both inside and outside the home. You want to be sure that any toxic plant is out of the chewing range of your dog. You can find out which toxic plants are in your area by contacting your veterinarian and local poison control center. Although young puppies are more likely to chew things than adults, you should be mindful of adult dogs who will often chew things that they should not. If you suspect that your dog has eaten or ingested a toxic plant, call your veterinarian or poison control center right away. You should not wait for the dog to show symptoms. Here is a brief list of some common plants to look out for:

Check the plants around your house to be sure they are not toxic.

- Anemone
- Azaleas
- Betel nut
- Bittersweet
- Buckeye
- Calla lily
- Crocus
- Daffodil
- Delphinium
- Daphne
- Holly berries
- Horsetail reed
- Hydrangea
- Iris
- Ivy of any type
- Jasmine
- Lantana camara
- Larkspur
- Lily of the valley
- Marijuana
- Mistletoe
- Morning glory
- Mushrooms of any type
- Oleander
- Palm
- Periwinkle
- Philodendron
- Poison Oak
- Poppy
- Primrose
- Rhododendron
- Rosary pea
- Sweet pea
- Tobacco
- Tulip
- Water hemlock
- Wisteria
- Yew

Chemicals Around the House and Yard

You want to be careful about weed killers, fertilizers, snail bait, pesticides, and any other chemicals that you may be using in your own yard. Most chemical fertilizers are toxic to animals in general. Because your Puggle is small and has a hound tendency to sniff everything, it could easily breathe in significant amounts of any weed killer or fertilizer that you may have used. It may also get sick from eating the treated grass. In the house and garage, you want to look out for antifreeze, rat poison, pine oil, perfumes, medications, chocolate, onions, electrical cords, and the like. If you have a cat, it probably likes to play with some of these things and can knock them off the counter onto the floor where your dog can easily get to them. It is recommended to place hazardous chemicals up high and out of reach or to use childproof locks on cabinets that your dog may get into. Your Puggle can easily learn to open the cabinet door under the kitchen sink or in the bathroom.

EVERYDAY CARE
OF YOUR PUGGLE

Now that you have brought your new Puggle home, it is time to establish a regular routine that works for both of you. A little planning can really go a long way in getting things off to a good start between you and your new Puggle. You will both have something to look forward to when there is a regular routine.

Feeding and Diet

Initially, the best way to choose the type of food for your Puggle is to check with the breeder where you obtained your puppy. You should try not to alter or change the existing diet. Doing so could result in diarrhea and other digestive problems, which can be serious in young puppies. Diarrhea in young puppies can dehydrate them very rapidly and cause severe problems or even death in extreme cases if not caught in time. Should you need to change your puppy's diet for any reason, do it gradually. Begin by substituting a few tablespoons of the new food for the old. Then gradually increase the percentage of new food until you have transitioned entirely to it.

Dogs are creatures of habit, and your Puggle will enjoy participating in a regular routine with you.

Because the nutritional needs of a dog can change throughout its lifetime, you need to consider some things when choosing a food. Puppies and adolescent dogs will require significantly higher amounts of nutrients, proteins, and calories than adult dogs. Their growing bodies demand a higher intake due to their rapid development in these early stages. Older dogs that are less active do not require as much protein or fat as growing, active dogs. By feeding your new Puggle a good quality food that is designed for its age and activity level, you are doing your part to ensure proper development. Most commercial dog food manufacturers are aware of this and package their food by growth stages and activity level.

You should feed your new puppy a diet that primarily consists of dry food. Using dry food has advantages over using moist or canned dog food. By going with the dry kibble, you are ensuring a chewing action, which is good for your Puggle's teeth and gums. Dry food is also less expensive than an equal quantity of canned food. You can supplement with

canned food from time to time in small amounts to stimulate your Puggle's appetite or add weight as needed.

Feeding schedule: A good rule of thumb is to feed your puppy three times a day: at morning, at midday, and at evening. Make sure that you have fresh water available at all times throughout the day as well. How much should you feed your dog at each meal? Ask your veterinarian for his or her daily recommendation. Feed one-third of that each of the three meals. For example, if your veterinarian says to feed your puppy 1 cup (275 ml) per day, then give your Puggle 1/3 cup (92 ml) three times a day. Do not leave food in the bowl all day long. Instead, give equal portions at three different intervals at the same time everyday. This will give your new puppy something to look forward to and will assist in proper development.

Portions: Because Puggles come in various sizes and are also big eaters, your portions will have to be monitored and may need to be adjusted accordingly. If you find that your puppy is finishing all three of the portions during the day and its body appears to be growing properly, then you can continue with these amounts. If your puppy appears to be gaining excessive weight, then you can reduce the amounts given. If the puppy is finishing its portions and its body appears thin, then you can increase the amounts of food given daily. Finally, if your Puggle has lots of energy and shows good muscle tone, is at the correct weight, and has a thick and shiny coat, then you are feeding it properly. Remember that the quality of a dog's diet will show in its condition and vitality.

Be sure to feed your Puggle a quality food.

Exercise and Playtime

The Puggle is content participating with both an active lifestyle as well as lounging around the house like a couch potato. If your own exercise routine consists of walking a few miles a day or just taking a leisurely stroll around the block, then the Puggle is a good choice for you. The Puggle is not a breed that will require you to spend a lot of time exercising it. However, this does not mean that your Puggle would not benefit from a daily stroll around the park. On the contrary, your Puggle will thoroughly enjoy the idea of going on a daily walk with you. Because of the Beagle mix, the Puggle will require more exercise than a Pug would. As with most canines, the Puggle needs daily exercise to keep physically fit and to stay mentally healthy. Regular exercise is also great for burning calories and increasing muscle mass as well as for increasing cardiovascular strength. On the other hand, not having enough exercise, when coupled with boredom, can lead to destructive behavior. A regular dose of supervised fun and games will usually satisfy many of your puppy's urges to chew, dig, and chase.

During the early puppy stages, your Puggle will not require a lot of exercise. If you have children or another dog in the house during these puppy stages, then your Puggle may be getting all the exercise it needs. A few outings to explore the backyard throughout the day for 10–15 minutes at a time are also recommended. Keep in mind that it is not advisable to take your dog for walks in public until its vaccinations are complete and your veterinarian gives you the all clear. As your puppy reaches the adolescent stage, around six months, it will begin to require more exercise than it did as a puppy. This is a good time to begin spending

Puggles are great with kids.

This Puggle loves to fetch the ball.

more quality time with your Puggle. This daily routine will help to solidify a bond between you and your puppy that will help you to enjoy each other's company for many years to come.

Your new exercise routine should start slow and gradually increase over time. You can begin by taking a stroll around the neighborhood on-leash for about 20–25 minutes. If you keep this regimen going and gradually increase the level, you can easily work up to 1 mile (1.6 km) a day at a reasonable pace. Keep in mind that this will be a new experience for your puppy, and it may want to stop and sniff at every opportunity. Your Puggle may also want to pull constantly in a direction that was not part of your plan. This will pass over time as your dog becomes familiar with the neighborhood. Walks are good opportunities for your Puggle to experience new stimuli, which include meeting other dogs and coming

into contact with new strangers. This exposure will help your dog develop its socialization skills and become well-adjusted, which helps to avoid problem behavior. Keep in mind that not everyone likes dogs as much as you, so it is important to respect others' feelings and maintain control of your puppy at all times.

Exercise can come in many forms. Each Puggle's exercise needs will vary depending on its age, sex, level of health, and the dog's own desires. You want to try out a few different activities and see what your dog seems to gravitate toward. Some examples would be on-leash jogging, race walking, playing Frisbee, or even the classic fetch. By having some Beagle heritage, many Puggles will enjoy playing a game of fetch with some type of toy or ball. This can be both satisfying and tiring for you and your dog, so you want to start slowly and build up some stamina. If your dog is at the point where it is pretty good with your training commands, then a trip to your local dog park is a great idea to get some exercise. Puggles love to run and play off-leash in an environment that is fenced and safe. In this case, you can choose to participate or just sit on a park bench and enjoy the show.

Handling and Socialization

By nature, the Puggle is an easygoing and happy dog that usually loves everybody. However, you want to make sure that you accommodate its natural instincts by ensuring it gets accustomed to being touched all over its body, meeting new dogs and people, and becoming familiar with various everyday events. Things

Taking your dog for a daily walk is recommended.

Here is a pack of Puggles on the move.

like traffic, strange noises, loud children, and unfamiliar animals can be intimidating to your puppy for the first few times. The goal is to introduce your new puppy gradually to as many of these new situations as you can. You should make a habit of taking your Puggle along with you as often as you can once it has received all its shots. You will find that your Puggle can be a real crowd pleaser and will enjoy all the attention that it gets.

Handling your puppy is an important part of your relationship together. Hopefully your breeder has done a good job in the early stages, which allows you to pick up where he or she left off. It is important that you regularly touch your dog on all parts of its body. Try to make an effort to handle your dog's ears, face,

Loud noises like traffic and children playing can be intimidating to your new puppy the first few times.

mouth, feet, tail, toenails, and the pads of its feet. Also, you will want to get your puppy used to rolling over on its back and its side, as well as allowing you to hold it in your arms. This will ensure that it will get used to being handled and will allow grooming and other activities

Be sure to socialize your Puggle with other dogs.

to go much smoother. It will also make things easier for your veterinarian to check your dog's body for problems and administer medications as needed. Be sure that you make every effort to reward your Puggle for allowing you to come into its personal space. In time, you will find that your Puggle will come to enjoy the physical contact.

As soon as your new puppy is old enough and has its shots, you should start bringing it outside of the house. You can begin by taking it for walks around the block, to the local dog park on a leash, to a playground where children are playing (if allowed at the playground), and so on. The key is to find a place that has a lot of activity where your dog feels safe.

Another great thing you can do is to enroll your Puggle in a local puppy socialization class.

They will usually allow your dog to begin from 11–16 weeks of age. You can usually find a class at your local humane society or other dog-training facilities. This is a nice, safe, monitored environment that will expose your new puppy to many different breeds of dog that are in its age range. If your puppy is active and a real go-getter, then it will be placed with the bigger dogs to run around freely. If, on the other hand, your Puggle is timid and scared of the other dogs, it will be placed into a more confined area with other dogs that have a similar disposition. You will find that if your puppy is initially shy, after a few weeks it will develop into a confident extrovert and become comfortable around other people and dogs. You will find that these classes can be very helpful in a short period of time.

You should start bringing your puppy outside of the house as soon as it is old enough and has had all its shots.

The Puggle is a fairly low-maintenance dog when it comes to grooming and hygiene. A good preventive measure for your Puggle's overall health is maintaining a weekly routine of grooming and good hygiene practices. Start the grooming process early in your puppy's young life. Have a full grooming session with your Puggle once a week, consisting of brushing its coat and teeth and checking its ears, eyes, nails, and underbelly. If your new Puggle does not like to be touched in certain areas while handling, try giving it a treat. Over time, your Puggle will relax and allow you to perform your regular maintenance duties.

Brushing

This can be one of the best monitors of your dog's overall health. The condition of the coat and skin and the feel of

Regular grooming of your Puggle will minimize shedding in your house.

the body is a good indicator of its health. Grooming can aid you in discovering small lumps that may appear under the skin or any rashes beginning to develop. Early detection of any condition is always the key.

Regular brushing removes dead hair and stimulates the dog's natural oils to add shine and maintain a healthy-looking coat. A natural bristle brush with medium to soft bristles should be used. You can also use a hound glove, a square-shaped mitten with short bristles on one side.

Find an elevated area like a grooming table, countertop, or bench. Have the puppy secured by your other hand in case the puppy tries to jump, potentially injuring itself. As you are brushing, be sure to pet and talk to your puppy. As you are stroking, go in the direction of the hair and not against it. Take care not to force the brush down too hard to avoid hurting your puppy. Make sure to brush behind the ears, up and down the tail, and around the feet.

Brushing the Teeth

To help prolong the health of your dog's mouth, regular brushing of the teeth is recommended by most veterinarians. This becomes more important as the dog ages and the teeth and gums become

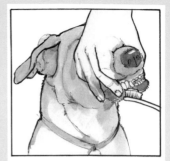

Oral hygiene is as important for the pet as it is for the owner.

more susceptible to decay. Use a baby toothbrush, or one designed specifically for dogs, and canine toothpaste that can be found at your local veterinarian or pet store. Do not use human toothpaste because it may be toxic to your dog.

Brushing your dog's teeth is very similar to brushing your own. Start by brushing from the dog's gum toward the tooth tip to avoid pushing any tartar underneath the gums. Bad breath is usually the result of tartar buildup on the teeth and a sign that you may need to start brushing more often. Inspecting the mouth regularly and checking for abnormal formations can help with early detection of infection and dental abscesses. Dogs are subject to infections and gum disease, too. Your dog's teeth should also be checked and cleaned by your veterinarian every six months or so.

Keeping the Eyes Clean

Another important weekly task is keeping the eyes clean. Puggles, like Pugs, can sometimes require special attention with their eyes. A small amount of discharge in the corner of the eye is pretty normal. If it becomes thicker and mucus-like in consistency, this may be a sign of an eye infection that needs medical attention. Most minor injuries to the eye can heal quickly if treated right away. Get a warm, damp cloth and wipe whatever discharge is evident every couple of days. Special wipes are also available that you can get from your veterinarian or pet supply store. Wiping the eyes regularly will prevent any buildup that may overlap with what has already dried and possibly lead to more serious issues.

Keeping the Ears Clean

The Puggle's ears will need to be cleaned and monitored on a regular basis. Breeds having pendulous ears are more prone to ear problems. If you live in a damp or wooded area, you will probably need to clean your Puggle's ears more often. This should be done with a cotton ball and special cleaner or powder that is made for dogs. Your dog is less likely to develop any serious ear problems if the ears remain clean. You can spot any developing problems as you are cleaning. If your Puggle is shaking its head or scratching its ears, this may be an indication of a problem. If the puppy shows signs of discomfort when you are touching its ears or when they are being scratched, this may call for a trip to the veterinarian. If your dog's ears are very dirty and require daily cleaning, this may be a sign of a greater problem beyond the normal buildup of dirt and ear wax.

Keeping the Nails Trimmed

Get your Puggle used to having its nails trimmed at an early age. They not only look nicer, but trimmed nails won't wreck furniture or scratch someone unintentionally. Older dogs with long nails may develop difficulty walking because as the nail grows longer, the only way to retain balance is to spread the toes apart, which causes the foot to flatten. Keep the nails short enough that they do not touch the ground as the dog is walking.

Before you cut the nail, make sure you are able to identify the quick, a blood vessel that runs through the nail and grows close to the end. If it is cut, it will bleed and be painful for the dog. Clip only a little of the nail at a time, especially if the nail is dark and the quick is hard to see. Do not panic if you happen to cut the quick. Just stop the bleeding with a clotting agent or towel, and speak soothingly to your dog. You may have to suspend your clipping routine until the dog settles down. You will become better at clipping as time goes on.

Bathing

Semiregular bathing is an essential component in your preventive health routine, helping maintain a shiny coat while removing any buildup that can lead to rashes or staph infections. Start bathing your dog as early as possible so that it becomes second nature to your Puggle. Otherwise, bath time can turn into a big, soapy mess.

Brushing your Puggle before a bath is your best bet to remove any dead hair and dust. Make sure the water temperature is suitable for your pup and that it has a nonslip surface to stand on. Wet the dog's coat with warm water, apply a shampoo approved for dogs, and work the shampoo into the coat and skin all the way down its body. Try to wash the head last so you don't get shampoo into its eyes while washing the body. Do not be surprised if your dog shakes out its coat during the bath. Finally, rinse the entire coat thoroughly, squeeze the excess water out of its coat, and dry the dog with a thick towel.

TRAINING TIPS

*Training your dog is one of the most
important aspects of ownership.
A puppy that is well-trained,
behaves itself around guests,
and has a good nature is always
a pleasure to be around. On
the other hand, a dog that is
not trained and has behavioral
problems is the number one reason
that pet owners give up their dogs
to shelters or worse.*

The Basic Commands

Early training with your new puppy is a vital part of owning a dog. During this time you will begin to establish what is expected of your dog and who the boss is. During the early puppy stages, all dogs should be taught the four basic commands. These are *sit, stay, lie down,* and *off.* Basic leash training is also recommended at an early age. By starting early, you are setting the stage for good socialization and advanced learning should you choose to go beyond the basics. The four basic techniques are dog friendly and easy to teach to practically any healthy dog.

The mood you are in and the training environment are important parts of having a good

*This Puggle has been housebroken
using the crate method.*

training session. You should never begin a session if you are irritated, preoccupied, or in distress. Your dog is sensitive to your human feelings and may associate your negative feelings with its training session. Also be sure that the training environment is not one where the Puggle will be easily distracted. An empty kitchen floor is a great place to start where there are no toys around or other distractions. Any place will do as long as there is not anything that will interfere with your puppy's concentration.

A puppy has a short attention span, so you should keep the training sessions short and to the point. You will maximize your success by keeping the sessions no more than 10–15 minutes. The goal is to make the experience enjoyable for you and your Puggle. Once your Puggle learns the basic commands in your quiet area with some success, you can then begin testing the puppy out in public.

Be sure to start with the basic commands.

Sit

The *sit* command is pretty easy to teach, and you can start as early as the second day of your puppy's arrival. First, get your puppy's attention with a treat you know it likes. You may also use your dog's kibble and combine an eating session with a training session. This works best if you are kneeling or sitting at the dog's level. Then hold the treat in front of your dog's nose and allow your Puggle to lick it but not to take it from you. Then gradually raise the treat, just above the level your pup would be in for sitting, and give the *sit* command. You want the dog to look up at the treat. It is unnatural for a dog to look up in a standing position, so the natural instinct is to sit to get a better look. As your Puggle bends its knees to maintain balance, it will assume the *sit* position. When this happens, release the treat to your puppy and praise it lavishly with praises like, "Good dog! Good girl! Good sit!" You want to be as enthusiastic as possible because dogs like to get verbal praises from their owners. Dogs enjoy being proud of themselves for accomplishing a good behavior in the pursuit of pleasing their owners.

Spend the Time to Train

Too many dog owners are unwilling to put in the necessary time needed to train their dogs properly. Many dog owners have the mistaken belief that dog training is difficult or unnecessary. Nothing could be further from the truth. Today's modern psychological training methods are fast, effective, and easy.

Puggles really strive to gain their owner's approval and to please their masters. This trait will go a long way in making the training process enjoyable. However, before you can start having fun training your puppy, you will need to know where and how to begin. You will need to learn:

- The basic commands
- The keys to potty training or housebreaking
- The differences between crate training, paper training, and litterbox training
- A dog's body language and communication methods
- How to address nuisance behaviors

Begin with the sit *command.*

Because the *sit* position is so natural for a dog, your dog may take a little time to associate the *sit* command with that action. Keep in mind that you will not have to use a treat forever in order to get your puppy to obey you. It is only used in teaching new behaviors until the dog has really learned the command. Eventually you will wean your pup off the treats and continue with verbal praise. Consistency is always the key. If you are diligent with your training, your dog will learn to sit on command.

Down or Lie

Teaching the *down* or *lie* command is probably as easy as the *sit* command when you understand how your puppy perceives this position. For a dog, the *down* position is a submissive one. So you do not want to force the dog down. By using a forceful method, the dog may develop a fear of the *down* command and run away from your session. You want to use a technique that enables the dog to go to the *down* position voluntarily and submit.

You can start off by using the *sit* command and having your dog assume that position. Then allow the dog to sniff or lick the treat but not take it from you. Then slowly start to bring the treat down toward the ground and use the *down* or *lie* command.

*The **down** position is a submissive one for your Puggle.*

Be consistent. Do not switch between saying "*Down!*" and saying "*Lie!*" It may take a few times, so try to use a treat that you know your dog really wants. As soon as your dog assumes that *down* position where the front paws are in front and the belly is touching the ground, release the treat and begin the verbal praises as before. Continue with the technique several times until your puppy associates lying down with getting a treat. The great thing about Puggles is that they are led by their nose and will usually follow the treat.

Once you feel like your Puggle has mastered this command, you can combine it with the *sit* command and alternate back and forth between the two commands. Try to catch your Puggle off guard when it is playing and shows no sign of lying down. Also, try to get it to remain in the *down* position for a longer period of time before releasing the treat. This will work in conjunction with the upcoming *stay* command.

Stay

The *stay* command is relatively easy to teach once your Puggle has learned the first two commands. It can be used in conjunction with these and can be called a *sit/stay* or *down/stay* command. Just as before, this command will be used with food and praise as the basis for motivation.

When teaching the *sit/stay*, start by having the dog sit next to you on your left. You will have the treat away from the dog in your right hand. Then reach across your body and place the food at the dog's nose. Next, give the *stay* command, step out with your right foot, and pivot your body as you move the treat directly in front of the dog as it is licking the treat in your hand. Be sure to keep your Puggle's head facing forward to maintain the *sit* position. Count to five or six and then move back to your original position with the dog on your left. When you return to your position you can release the food and give praises to the dog.

To teach the *down/stay*, you want to start by having your dog assume the *down* position to the left of your body. After the dog lies down, say "*Stay,*" step out, and pivot with your right foot as before. Give a count of six and return to your original position. Then release the treat and praise the dog again. After about a week or so of doing this, you should try to increase the distance between you and your dog. When you pivot to face your Puggle, give the command "*Stay*" and then take a few steps back. Then

The stay command is next in the lineup.

return to your original position and give the treat as before.

Off

Please note that some trainers use the *down* command for getting the dog to stop jumping on you. If you choose to use *down* for this command, then you can use *lie* when getting the dog to lie down. The *off* command can be a little trickier to teach than the previous three commands. This is because of a dog's natural tendency to jump up on you out of excitement. Nevertheless, it is an essential command to learn, especially when meeting strangers. Many people are not sympathetic to an untrained puppy and can be less than thrilled to have a puppy jumping up on them. If you want to increase your chances of teaching this command to your puppy then you must never reward your puppy for jumping up on you. This can be tough love for some owners who feel that it is so cute to have the puppy jumping up on them. Trying to get a dog to stop jumping after it was allowed to jump as a puppy is much more difficult to break than having never allowed it to jump up in the first place.

When the puppy comes up to greet you, the goal is to get it to stop in front of you without making an attempt to jump up on you. When the Puggle tries to jump on you, time things so that it will miss you as you step back and say "*Off.*" By doing this, your pup will having nothing to prop up on and should return to a standing position with all fours on the ground. Another method would be to bend down and stick out your knee so it makes contact with your Puggle's chest and causes it to fall back. Again, you will quickly use the *off* command as it is making a jump attempt. In either case, the goal is to make the act of jumping up a negative one, which has no reward. When your dog is down, you can give praises.

The key to this command is to have cooperation among the other members of your household. If one person is allowing the dog to jump up, this will sabotage your efforts and send a mixed signal that confuses your puppy.

Leash Training

You should definitely get your puppy accustomed to wearing a collar and leash as early as possible. Usually somewhere between eight to ten weeks of age is best. You will start with the collar and put it onto the puppy as soon as possible so

These three Puggles know the sit command very well.

it gets used to the collar. You can then attach a nametag or license to the collar for identification purposes. The collar should fit comfortably and not too loosely, which may allow it to be pulled over the head. The puppy will complain in protest initially. After a few days, your pup will not even realize that it is there.

Once your Puggle is used to the collar, attach a small leash while you are playing with the puppy. Do not try to lead your dog around just yet. It needs to get used to having something attached to the collar. Just let it drag the leash around the house for a while. The puppy may tug, chew, or paw at the leash until it realizes

that the leash is not a threat. You should attach the leash a few times a day for the next couple of days. Having the leash drag around is a great way to make small corrections to where the puppy is not allowed to visit. As your Puggle attempts to go to an off-limits area, simply step on the leash and say "No."

When you are ready to begin training, put the leash on and allow the puppy to lead you around the house for the first few times. You can apply minimal pressure, but you should never jerk or pull on the puppy. These initial training sessions should be kept short until the puppy is unconcerned about having the leash around its neck. Next, try to get your puppy to follow you as you move away. If your pup is not interested, then try using a treat of some kind. Hold the treat in front of its nose to encourage the Puggle to follow you. When it makes the first few steps in your direction, you should then praise continually as you continue moving back. Once you feel that the sessions are going well inside the house, you can move into the backyard and gradually increase the time spent on the lesson. Pretty soon you will be able to move to the front of the house and eventually take a walk down the street, once your puppy has all of its shots.

When you begin taking walks down the street, you will find that your puppy will want to walk in front of you or fall behind because of a curious scent. This is normal and you should freely allow this to occur for the first five to ten walks. Eventually, the goal is to have your dog walking at your pace on your left-hand side. As the pup lunges forward to pull away from you, just give a firm tug and say "*Heel.*" You never want to cause the dog pain or lift it into the air when doing this. You are just trying to get it to associate some discomfort when an attempt to lunge or pull is made. When the puppy returns to your side, be sure to praise and reward your pup. The key to this lesson is to keep the lessons short while continually making adjustments. You also want to try to be patient with your Puggle during this time.

Housebreaking

The main goal of housebreaking is to teach your dog to relieve itself in the proper area that you designate. Being consistent and giving praise will help to attain this. The consistency

Here are two Puggles ready to take their walk.

will begin by feeding the puppy at the same time everyday and with the same food. Young puppies are susceptible to a changing diet. A change in food and feeding time can negatively affect their digestive system, which will cause setbacks to your housebreaking efforts.

Along with the regular feedings, you will need to have regular outings that provide your Puggle with an opportunity to relieve itself. Regular feedings and outings depend on each other and should be combined consistently. This is because a feeding will usually be a trigger for an outing shortly thereafter. Much praise should then be given to reward the puppy for going at the appropriate time. This praise will help the dog to understand the desired behavior. Corrections, like praise, should also be used when your puppy relieves itself in an inappropriate location. These corrections must be done at the precise time when the undesired action occurs.

Whether you are giving praise or corrections, you cannot allow any time to pass after the act has occurred. If any time passes, then you will fail to deter or reinforce the action, and your puppy will become confused. Most dogs do not have the ability to associate a correction with an action that occurred in the past. So scolding a dog that soiled an area in your absence will not have any effect.

One common mistake made during housebreaking is starting too early and expecting too much. Almost no puppy has the physical ability to be housebroken any earlier than three months of age. Very few puppies even have this ability before the age of four months. In these early months, the puppy simply is not able to control its bladder and sphincter muscles. Any attempt to override this limitation is futile and may cause bigger problems down the road.

Do not be one of the many new dog owners who try to start too early. Doing this will only lead to frustration and possibly insurmountable future training setbacks. These premature corrections can be a detriment to the ongoing psycho-

logical development of your Puggle and rob it of any sense of worth. There are better ways to approach these early stages of development in regard to housebreaking. The three methods we will be covering are crate training, paper training, and litterbox training. Each one of these methods has merit and is individually suited to your specific circumstances as an owner.

Crate Training

The vast majority of trainers today are big advocates of using the crate as a primary means of housebreaking. The use of a crate is a great way to condition a sense of routine in a young puppy, which in turn will also reduce the time needed for a young puppy to become housetrained. This is because all dogs are creatures of habit, and so their natural instincts become complementary when combined with the consistent training of a crate. Many first-time dog owners are reluctant to use the crate method because they believe that locking up a dog for any length of time is cruel. As humans, we lock up our criminals in small cages as a form of punishment, but dogs view the cage as a den and a safe place of their own. In fact, crate training will actually add a sense of comfort and help to build confidence in a young puppy. Since puppies usually sleep most of the day, having a safe and quiet place is important to them.

The crate itself should only be large enough for the puppy to stand up, lie down, or stretch out in comfortably. You do not want to start with a crate that is too big because the puppy may sleep in one area and relieve itself in the other. The main idea behind crate training is that Puggles are generally clean animals and are reluctant to eliminate where they sleep. By itself, this natural instinct to be clean is not

The crate will become a comfort zone and safe place for your puppy.

enough to become housebroken. You must clean up any accidents as soon as possible. If not, the puppy may start to think that going in its crate is the desired behavior.

For optimum results, introduce and acclimate your Puggle to the crate as early as possible before starting the housebreaking process. Try to place the crate in a dry, warm, comfortable location that is away from any loud noises or other distractions. For added comfort, you can place a blanket, a favorite toy, and a safe dog chew in or near the crate area. Take care not to allow too much clutter into the crate area. You want the puppy to feel like this is a space that it can stretch out and be comfortable in. Be

sure that the room is temporarily isolated from any other animals or competitive dogs.

Initially, confine the new puppy to a small area. If your area is larger than a laundry room, you may want to use a 4 foot (120 cm) by 6 foot (180 cm) playpen to surround the crate. Be sure to leave the door open to the crate so the puppy can freely wander in and out, especially at night. The idea is for the puppy to go into the crate for naps and to relax and then come into the open area to relieve itself. You then want to start locking the puppy in the crate for five-minute intervals while you are present. Once the time has passed, let the puppy out and give much praise. Do this a few times a day and then gradually increase the time in the crate over a period of days. Once you have reached the half-hour mark in your presence, you should then return to five-minute intervals while you are away. At any point during these sessions, it is likely that your puppy will whine.

Do not give in but rather, allow the puppy to get used to being in the crate for an extended period of time.

In these early months, you can take your puppy outside to relieve itself upon awakening from a nap as this is when it will most likely have to go. However, do not expect too much in the way of being housebroken as your Puggle is still too young to control its organs. Be patient in these early stages while your puppy is becoming acclimated. In time, your puppy will settle down and become very comfortable in its crate.

Once your dog reaches about the four-month mark and is used to its crate, you can then begin the real housebreaking process. This can be a relatively easy process if you are committed and follow a strict routine. A daily schedule should be drawn up that includes all the important daily activities like feeding, walks, exercise, playtime, and crate time. An example would look something like the following:

- 6:30 wake up and take puppy out for potty
- 6:45 feed the puppy while cleaning the crated area
- 7:00 take puppy outside for another potty or go for a walk with puppy
- 7:30 have some playtime while getting ready for work
- 8:00 lock puppy in crate and go to work
- 12:00 come home for lunch, feed puppy while cleaning puppy's area, play with puppy, take the puppy out for potty or for a short walk, eat own lunch

- 12:45 put puppy back in crate and return to work
- 5:20 return from work and let puppy out for potty
- 5:30 feed puppy and clean crated area
- 5:45 take puppy for a longer walk
- 6:15 eat own dinner and then spend some quality time with dog
- 7:30 try some basic training with dog and then allow supervised playtime
- 9:30 maybe give a biscuit or other dog treat
- 10:30 take dog out for last potty or short walk
- 11:00 place dog in the crate for the night

This is a good example of a reasonable schedule for proper crate training. Feel free to use this as a guide to create a routine that best fits your schedule. The most important thing to remember is to follow whatever schedule you set from one day to the next. Also, you want to try to continue with the schedule through the weekend. If you are diligent and follow your schedule closely for at least 40 days, you will have great results and have a dog that is properly housebroken in no time.

Keep in mind that crate training is not suitable for everyone. It works best for owners who are going to keep their dog primarily indoors and allow the dog to relieve itself in the backyard or while taking a walk. It also works well for dogs that will be outside or in the garage during the day and spend their nights indoors. Crate training is probably not the best method to use if you do not have the time to commit to the training schedule. It also may not be the best method if your dog is going to be solely an indoor dog and is not going to be let out frequently to go potty. If that is the case, you may want to consider paper or litter box training as a primary method.

Paper Training

Paper training is one of the oldest and most used methods of housebreaking available. Among the benefits are its cost effectiveness and its simplicity. Paper training seems to come naturally to most dog owners. This is probably due to the fact that it was the preferred method of your parents and their parents. All that is really required for this method is some old newspaper, an enclosed area of the home, a little time, and some patience. One of the advantages of paper training, compared with crate training, is that the procedure requires significantly less time for the owner. The routine of paper training is also the most flexible of the training methods. There is no wonder why it is still the most commonly utilized method of housebreaking today.

You may be asking yourself, "Why bother with crate training if this is so easy and doesn't take up as much of my time?" There are some disadvantages that you should be aware of before making your final decision. Research has shown that paper training teaches some dogs that it is acceptable to relieve themselves in the house. The dog may learn that it should go only on the paper and not outside. Some dogs have been taken on long walks without once relieving themselves. Then once they got back into the house, they immediately went for the paper to do their business. This can make it difficult for the owner who continues to use the paper as a training method. Sometimes giving excessive praise when the puppy goes indoors and not enough while on the walk can cause this problem.

Another problem with paper training is that it may condition the dog to think going in the house is acceptable as long as it goes on some

Paper training is a reliable method that has been around for decades.

paper. The dog may go both indoors and outdoors since it is conditioned and praised when going in either location. Since there have been no accidents, the perception of the owner is that the dog is finally housebroken. The problem arises when the owner takes away the paper. Then one day, some important papers are left on the floor in the den or living room, and the dog relieves itself on the papers. The reality is that the dog was never fully housebroken in this scenario. It may now take some time to train the dog not to go on papers, which can take longer than the housebreaking process itself. In this case, using the crate-training method may have been better.

Litterbox Training

Litterbox training is an entirely different approach than crate training or paper training. The idea here is to condition the dog to believe it is perfectly acceptable to go in the house as long as it goes in the designated area. This area

This Puggle enjoys hanging out in a cat tree.

of newspaper. While the puppy is in its area, the owner should be nearby to observe and give praise when the dog goes anywhere on the paper. This will condition the dog to believe that going on the paper pleases its owner. After some time when you are sure the dog will go only on the paper, you can begin to gradually reduce the size of the area and begin to expose the floor. After some time, the only place left for the puppy to go is in the litterbox. Throughout this process, be sure to make verbal corrections when the dog relieves itself anywhere except in the desired area.

If your preference is for the dog to go only inside at the designated location, praise should only be given when this occurs. You may wonder why some might want their dog to go only inside if they also allow it to play outside. One reason is that they may have children at play and do not want the yard to be full of waste that can be tracked into the house. Another reason is that some owners prefer to maintain a very well manicured lawn that is free of dog waste. Additionally, the owner may not want to have to pick up after the dog in public locations. Most public places now require you to carry doggy bags and clean up after your animal. If any of these reasons is a factor for you, then litterbox training should be the training method of choice.

Keep in mind that litterbox training has the same potential restrictions and potential problems as paper training. One additional problem for the litterbox-only dog is that it does not have an opportunity to exercise its instinctual need to mark territory. This is a dog's primary

can be an actual litterbox, a corner in the garage, or on some newspaper in a specific area. The dog can be taught to go both in the box and outside or just solely in the box. Like the other methods, litterbox training should not begin until the puppy is between four and six months of age. When starting, be sure to choose an area that is easily accessible, away from hazards, and free of distractions. Make sure this is the place where the litterbox is always going to be located until the housebreaking process is finished.

Begin by putting down newspaper in an area of about 6 feet (180 cm) by 8 feet (240 cm) if space is available. Then place the litterbox within this area and line it with the same type mode of social communication with other dogs. Scent marking can play a significant role in the social development of a dog and should not be totally eliminated from its routine. If the litter-box method is used, the dog should be allowed to urinate outside while keeping the fecal waste to the litterbox. You will need to make sure praise is given both inside and out in this case.

Addressing Nuisance Behaviors

As a new Puggle owner, you have chosen a dog that is known to have a good temperament. This will be your companion, your family member, your friend, and your protector. Although you have taken measures to obtain a dog with a good temperament, you have to remember that it is still a dog. You are bound to experience a behavioral problem of some type at some point throughout your journey. These types of problems are the number one reason that owners abandon their dogs, either through a new home, a shelter, or euthanasia. One key thing to remember is that dogs do not think like humans, and humans do not generally think like dogs. A dog has no chance of ever understanding the depths of the human mind, but a human can learn to understand how a dog sees the world and communicates. So it is up to you as the human to take the initiative and learn to think like a dog from time to time.

Since every dog is unique and every situation is unique, we will cover the basics of the most common nuisance behaviors. This will enable you to have a good chance of solving the problem yourself without having to bring in an expert or worse, abandoning your pet alto-gether. Having patience and understanding will

Your dog should look to you as the alpha leader of the pack.

go a long way when dealing with an undesired behavior. It is our hope that you will make a real effort should a problem arise.

A Dog's Language

It is generally accepted that dogs are descendents of the wolf. Like the wolf, a dog will look for the alpha leader of the pack for direction. Your dog should look to you to be that leader. If you fail to take on that role, your dog may replace you as the leader in its mind. This can become a problem in many households without the owner knowing.

Understanding and Speaking Dog

Some ways a dog expresses dominance:
- The dog aggressively makes eye contact.
- The dog displays dominance over other dogs by standing at right angles over them.
- The dog stands while keeping its ears and tail up and the hair on its neck raised.
- The dog is not willing to part with toys or other objects in its mouth.
- The dog is very possessive about the food bowl.
- The dog dislikes being petted.

Some ways a dog expresses submission:
- The dog crouches down with its ears back and tail pointing down between its rear legs.
- The dog avoids eye contact.
- The dog lies on its side with its rear legs in the air.

Some ways a human can express dominance:
- The human meets a nonaggressive dog's gaze.
- The human acts taller than the dog by using body language.
- The human ignores the dog's attempts to be sociable.
- The human takes over the dog's physical location when the animal performs an undesired act.

One way that an alpha leader establishes order is by using direct eye contact. You should immediately begin to practice this with your puppy, even if you have to hold its head still for ten seconds. Feel free to give your puppy a treat for participating in this exercise with you. You do not want the eye contact to be threatening in any way unless you are addressing an undesirable behavior. Never try to make eye contact with an older dog that may not have learned as a puppy that it is acceptable. This may be perceived as a threat and could trigger an aggressive outburst. Remember that all dogs have the potential for both dominant and submissive behavior. However, only a few dogs will exhibit any significant dominant behavior in their lifetime. This can be minimized if the owner establishes his or her dominance early on.

A dog will give you a sign that it wants to play by using the play bow. This is when the dog goes down on its front legs with the chest to the ground while the rear legs are elevated. Puppies will often do this with each other and play fight, which helps them learn the limits of biting. This will aid them as they get older and have interactions with other dogs. Be careful not to become falsely reassured by the playfulness of your puppy's aggression. If encouraged, excessive playful aggression can lead to more serious aggression as the dog ages. Do not participate in a tug-of-war with a toy or play fight with a puppy that shows early signs of dominant behavior. The checklist on the left shows how dogs communicate and how humans can respond.

Aggression

This can be one of the most common problems that concern dog owners. Although this behavior is not as common with a well-bred Puggle, it can occur in any dog. Some types of aggression include defensive, predatory, possessive, protective, fearful, noise provoked, and maternal. An aggressive dog may lunge, attack, or bite another person or dog. This type of behavior is dangerous and not to be tolerated at any time. Some other

Address nuisance behaviors early so you do not become one of the statistics who abandon their dog.

forms of mild aggression can be growling, posturing, and baring teeth. Although this type of aggression is not dangerous, it can be frightening and can lead to a more aggressive action if the cause is not ascertained.

Aggressive behavior is a sign of dominance, and the dog should not have a dominant role in your family. Do not challenge a dog while it is in an aggressive state as this may provoke an attack. Instead, try to isolate what is causing the fear, reassure the dog that this is not a threat, and gradually defuse the situation. Do not allow anyone else to come in contact with the dog at this point. See if you can redirect the behavior by getting the dog to sit or inviting it to play fetch with a toy. Then try to get the dog to sit and begin to pet it gently and

show it that everything is going to be fine. Then you may want to give the dog a treat as a reward for now having a calm disposition.

Barking

This is a dog's way of talking, and it usually has a reason. This can sometimes be frustrating because you may not know what the bark means. Some dog owners think that by encouraging their dog to bark, this will cause it to be a good watchdog. The truth is that most dogs will bark when a stranger is outside or comes to the door anyway.

Another common occurrence is when a new puppy barks or whines for the first few nights in a new home. Make sure not to go to it when this happens, as this will reinforce the unwanted

Barking is a dog's way of communicating and it usually has a cause.

behavior. Instead, try smacking the top of the crate and saying "*No*" or "*Quiet*" in a stern voice. The puppy will not enjoy the noise of banging on the crate and will usually refrain from this behavior after a few times.

Excessive barking can become a nuisance to a new owner and should be addressed right away. Sometimes it will involve some dedication on your part to solve the problem. The key is to observe the environment and try to discover the cause. Is the dog seeking attention? Does the dog think it's time to eat? Does the dog need to go out for potty? Is the dog being left alone? Ask yourself these questions and see if you can figure out the reason. Eventually, you

will get to know your dog's barks and will come to understand just what it wants. Fortunately, Puggles tend to use their barks for a reason and are not like many small, yapping dogs.

Jumping Up

For most dogs, jumping up is a sign of excitement and their friendly way of saying hello. Many dog owners are happy to have their dog jump up on them when they arrive home. The problem is that this warm welcome may not be appreciated when a guest comes over for a visit and is greeted in the same manner. You allow the puppy to jump up on you until about four months of age. If you make corrections too early, this could intimidate the puppy and cause it to be timid around humans later in life.

Once the dog is of age, you can begin to make the corrections as needed. Try using the *sit* command when the puppy attempts to jump up on you. Be sure to give praise and a treat to reinforce the good behavior. Make sure that all of other family members are on board with this correction. If your dog is older and has already picked up the habit of jumping up, you can try grasping its paws tightly and squeezing. Then give a stern "Off" command. Your Puggle will soon come to realize that this is unwelcome. Then be sure to give praise and lots of petting to reassure the dog that you are still glad to see it.

Biting

Most puppies in the early stages will try to bite or chew on your fingers, socks, clothing, and so on. This is a good time to show the puppy the biting boundaries. If the puppy bites your finger too hard, you can force your finger horizontally toward the back of the puppy's mouth, causing discomfort, and say "*Easy*" or

"*No bite*" to indicate you are being hurt. This can be accompanied by a scream or high-pitched squeal to let the puppy know that you have been hurt. Another thing you can do when the puppy is biting your finger is too pinch its bottom lip firmly. If the puppy does not respond to your correction attempts, you can always put it away for a time-out. The key is to teach your dog early on that biting is not an acceptable behavior.

If you have an older dog that is starting to exhibit a desire to bite, you must address the behavior as soon as possible. A bite from a mature dog can be more serious and can have costly repercussions, for you as the owner, should your dog bite another person. Most of the time, biting can easily be avoided by properly socializing your dog at an early age. You must introduce your dog to both humans and other dogs as often as you can. If it has been isolated, a dog can sometimes come to think that it is the only dog around and therefore may show aggressive behavior when it comes into contact with another dog.

Chewing

Chewing is one of the most common pastimes for a dog, and Puggles are no different. Almost every dog enjoys sinking its teeth into a tasty bone or anything else it thinks is chew worthy. Your job as the new owner is not to discourage the dog's natural urge to chew but, rather, to provide a suitable chewing device that is good for the dog's dental hygiene. Dogs have a need to exercise their jaws by chewing, to massage their gums, and to break in their new teeth. If you do not provide a safe chewing toy or treat, then your dog will find a nice piece of furniture, clothing or other thing to

Puppies have a need to exercise their jaws by chewing something.

wreck in your house to satisfy this need. You want to be sure to puppyproof your home as a precaution and put away personal items that you think may entice your puppy to chew.

If you happen to catch your puppy in the act, try to redirect it to a chew or other toy you may have purchased for it. There are several types of dog chews available on the market today. Some edible ones include pig ears, bully sticks, rawhide, greenies, and kong stuffers. Some chewable toys include nylabones, rope toys, kongs, frozen bones, and so on. Each dog has its particular likes and dislikes, so you will have to experiment with a few different ones until you stumble on a good one. The key is to find a chew that is enjoyed every time.

TRAVELING AND VACATIONS

Start getting your puppy accustomed to traveling as early as possible. Even if you do not plan on taking your Puggle with you when you travel, you will still have to bring it to the veterinarian, the kennel, or the pet sitter. In addition, do not forget to include a way of identifying your Puggle in case it gets lost.

Car Travel

You should get your puppy accustomed to riding in the car with you as early as possible. If you are able, try to take the dog in the car with you for small trips to the pet store. Many pet stores will allow you to bring the dog in with you to wander around. By taking these little rides to the store, your dog will begin to look forward to your short adventures together. This will begin to condition a positive experience while riding in the car. On the other hand, if you allow your dog to ride in the car only for a visit to the veterinarian, the dog may begin to associate the car with the negative experience of getting an injection. Many dogs are prone to getting carsick initially, so be sure you bring the dog on an empty stomach. Also, try to get your Puggle to relieve itself

Who could possibly go on vacation without taking this adorable puppy along?

before entering the car to avoid a nervous accident. Prepare for an accident by packing a leash, some paper towels, a potty pad, some clean-up solution, and a towel. This way you will not be caught off guard, which can also make the trip unpleasant for you.

Use a crate: The safest method for the dog to ride in the car is in its crate. If you already use a crate in the house, use the same crate in the car. By using a familiar environment, the dog will be less uneasy during the ride.

A helpful passenger: The close confinement of a crate can cause some dogs to become carsick. If this is the case, then you may want to bring a passenger with you and allow the dog to sit on his or her lap during the ride. This can also aid the dog into feeling more at ease in the presence of a familiar human.

Harness: Another option is to use a dog harness that is made specifically for car travel. This device comfortably straps your dog in, much

When flying with a pet, try to book a nonstop flight to minimize your dog's discomfort.

driving, you could become distracted and get into an accident.

Safety issues: If you have a truck, do not ever allow your dog to ride freely in the back unless he is securely attached to a very short lead. A longer lead is dangerous because it may allow the dog to fall out and be dragged should the truck have to stop suddenly. Never allow your dog to run loose in the car while wearing a collar and leash. Several dogs have killed themselves by hanging under these circumstances. The crate is a much safer place to leave your dog should you have go into the store alone. As common as it may be, do not allow your dog to stick its head out of an open window while the car is in motion. This is because foreign debris can get blown into the puppy's eyes and cause damage.

Never, ever: During warm weather, never leave your dog in the car unattended, even with the windows down. The temperatures in a car can easily reach over 100°F (37.8°C), which is very dangerous for a dog. Incidentally, in some states, it is a crime to leave your dog in your car unattended. You may also run the risk of having your Puggle stolen by dognappers.

Air Travel

In recent years, traveling with a dog by air has become much more convenient. Many airlines have made great strides trying to ensure your dog's trip is comfortable and safe. You will need to contact the airline in advance to find out what its policy is regarding dogs. Some airlines

like a seatbelt would a human. Do not allow the dog to roam freely about the car. This can be dangerous for both you and your dog. If you should have to stop suddenly, your dog could be thrown and injured. If your dog should suddenly start to climb on you or scratch you while will allow you to carry the dog with you onto the plane for an additional fee, while others prefer you check the dog into cargo.

If cargo is the choice you make, many airlines will not allow the dogs to fly if the temperature is going to be 85°F (29.4°C) or more at any location along the way. They are very strict with this rule to protect the animal's safety. One solution, if you are flying during the summer, is to book your flight in either the early morning or evening. The temperatures will usually cool down during these times in most areas. The airlines will require the dog to use a specified crate that is in compliance with their regulations. They will usually specify the crate's size, what material it should be made of, any special labeling needed, food and water dish requirements, a health certificate, and what to line the bottom with. You must comply with all that they ask or risk being turned away.

Your goal is to try to make the flying experience as comfortable as possible. You should place one of your Puggle's favorite toys in the crate. Try not to feed the dog for several hours before checking in. This will minimize the dog's need to relieve itself. If the airline required you to feed the animal before a long trip, try to keep the meal light. Try to book a nonstop flight to your location if at all possible. This will minimize the discomfort of your dog's experience and the chance of a transfer mixup. We all know how easy it is for our luggage to get lost. The hope is that an airline would take extra care to ensure that an animal is not separated from its owner, but you never know. For this reason, be sure that your dog is properly identified and your information appears on its identification tags and on the crate. Remember that your dog may be traveling on a different part of the

Always plan ahead when booking trips that include your dog.

plane than you, so every precaution should be taken to help minimize a mistake.

Trips and Vacations

You decide that you are going to take a family vacation and bring your Puggle with you. This is perfectly fine. However, you will need to make reasonable accommodations and book everything ahead of time. The last thing you want is to stop at a motel in the middle of the night and discover that they do not allow dogs. Additionally, you want to make sure that your ultimate destination also allows dogs. You would be surprised to find out that many well-known hotel and motel establishments are not canine friendly. You should mention that you will be keeping your dog crated while on the premises.

The Internet is a great place to search for dog-friendly overnight establishments. Some travel guides available in many pet stores highlight which hotels will accommodate dogs. These guides may also give you ideas of how to have fun while traveling with a dog as well as places to go that you may not have thought of.

Another consideration while traveling with your dog is the possible exposure to external parasites along the way. Some areas of the country can be infested with fleas, ticks, or germ-carrying mosquitoes. For this reason, it is a good idea to carry an array of various repellants. You want to be prepared even in the hotels that you choose. Remember that if they do allow dogs, chances are there have been other dogs in the room before yours.

If you are traveling by van or motor home, ensure your dog's safety by locking your vehicle securely when you leave. More than likely you will have valuables, and you will lock it anyway. However, a dog is probably the most valuable and difficult possession to replace, so make every effort to keep the Puggle safe. Along with locking the vehicle in your absence, be sure to provide adequate food, water, and ventilation for your dog. This may be the first time your dog has taken a road trip so be conscious of what its needs are. Do not leave your Puggle alone for any significant length of time as it is in a foreign place.

Boarding Kennels

If you decide not to bring your dog with you on vacation, then you will have to make alternate arrangements for it while you are away. You may be lucky enough to have a family member or a close neighbor that your dog can stay with in your absence. If not, then your next logical move would be to place your Puggle in a boarding kennel. Your veterinarian may be able to recommend a good kennel in your area. Some veterinarians may also have technicians that board their patients in their home or yours. This is not uncommon, so ask.

If you do choose to use a kennel, visit it in advance to do some investigating. Ask to take a tour of the facility and make note of the cleanliness where the dogs are kept. Try to talk to some of the employees and get a feel for how they treat the dogs. Be sure to ask lots of questions.
• Are the dogs played with?
• Do the employees spend any quality time with them?
• What is a typical day's activity schedule?
• What precautions are made for flea control?
• Do they require all dogs to be current on rabies and kennel cough vaccines?

A good kennel will see your concern and welcome your questions about its operation. Do not be shy. Remember that you are just trying to ensure that your dog is going to be as comfortable as possible while you are away.

Identifying Your Puggle

It is not something that most people want to consider, but your Puggle could someday become lost or stolen. At the very minimum, every dog should wear a collar with an identification tag. This is the first thing that strangers

Every dog should have a collar and ID tag.

would look for if they happen across a lost dog. You will want to inscribe the tag with your dog's name and your name and phone number. If the tag remains intact on the dog, it is the quickest way of identification. Unfortunately, puppies can easily slip out of collars, and the tags can fall off. This does not mean that you should not use the collar and tag system, though. You may want to supplement the iden-

tification of your new Puggle with a more permanent solution.

Tattoos: For years, many owners have chosen to place a tattoo on their dog. One way is to use a number with a registry. The problem with this method is that there are now several registries in operation that would have to be checked. The best solution for this is to list a long-term address or phone number. The tattoo

These three white-nosed Puggles have been microchipped.

is usually placed on the inside of your dog's rear thigh. This makes it easily noticed and does not require any sophisticated machinery to install or to read. This is a fairly painless procedure for your dog, but some do not really care for the buzzing sound much. On occasion, the tattoos are not legible and therefore need to be redone. Any stranger that may find a lost dog with a tattoo will usually inform a veterinarian or animal shelter, who will know what to do.

Microchips: The latest method of identifying your dog is called microchipping. The microchip is a miniature computer chip that stores a number with your dog's information. This is a rice-sized pellet that is inserted under the dog's skin at the base of the neck, between the shoulder blades. There is no discomfort for the dog during this procedure. This is a permanent identifier and will never be removed or get lost. If your dog happens to get lost and turns up at the humane society, they will be able to trace you by scanning the dog. These days, most veterinary offices and animal shelters have scanners that can read the microchips. Also, most scanners can read the different microchips that are available in the market today. This is quickly becoming the preferred method of identification used in the dog world. Many breeders are prechipping their puppies before you even take possession of the animal.

You would not want to lose such a beautiful dog as this one, so be sure your dog is properly identified.

Mixed Breed Organizations

American Canine Hybrid Club
10509 S & G Circle
Harvey, AR 72841
Phone: (479) 299-4415
http://www.achclub.com

Australian Labradoodle Association
   of America
http://www.australianlabradoodleaa.org

Cockapoo Club of America
31766 Oak Ranch Court
Westlake Village, CA 91361
www.cockapooclub.com

Designer Doggies
P.O. Box 750231
Petaluma, CA 94975
Phone: (415) 999-4114
www.designerdoggies.com

North American Maltipoo Club
www.maltipooclub.org

Puggle.org
www.puggle.org

Mixed Breed Books

Bobrowsky, Carol, Jim Gladden, and Mary
   Bloom, *Schnoodle*. Allenhurst, New Jersey:
   Kennel Club Books, 2006.
Fields-Babineau, Miriam, *Labradoodle*.
   Allenhurst, New Jersey: Kennel Club Books,
   2006.
Foley, Mary D., *Cockapoo*. Allenhurst, New
   Jersey: Kennel Club Books, 2006.
Lee, Kathryn, *Goldendoodle*. Allenhurst, New
   Jersey: Kennel Club Books, 2006.

Woolf, Norma Bennet, *Hot Dogs! Fourteen of
   the Top Designer Dogs*. Hauppauge, New
   York: Barron's Educational Series, Inc., 2006.

Magazines

Dog Fancy
P.O. Box 53264
Boulder, CO 80322-3264
Phone: (303) 666-8504

Dog World
500 N. Dearborn, Suite 1100
Chicago, IL 60610
Phone: (312) 396-0600

Animal Welfare Organizations

USA

American Society for the Prevention of
   Cruelty to Animals (ASPCA)
424 E. 92nd Street
New York, NY 10128-6804
Phone: (212) 876-7700
www.aspca.org

Australia

Royal Society for the Prevention of Cruelty
   to Animals (RSPCA) Australia, Inc.
P.O. Box 265
Deakin West, Act 2600
Phone: (02) 6282 8300
www.rspca.org.au

Canada

The Canadian Society for the Prevention of
   Cruelty to Animals (CSPCA)
5215 Jean-Talon O
Montreal, PQ, H4P 1x4
Phone: (514) 735-2711
www.spca.com

How cute are these two babies?

INDEX

Photo Credits
All interior photos by Chelle Calbert.

Cover Photos
All cover photos by Chelle Calbert.

Acknowledgments
The contents of this book come from my experience with the breed, independent research, various articles, breeders, veterinarians, and Puggle owners. I would like to thank the mad scientist breeder Wallace Havens for his contributions and decision to regularly put these two breeds together. I also want to thank the various Puggle owners for their suggestions and encouragement and allowing me to spend time with their dogs. Special thanks go to Gary Garner and the American Canine Hybrid Club for their ongoing support. I wish to extend my gratitude to my parents, who always believed in me and encouraged me to pursue my own goals without judgment. Thanks to my daughter, Devina, for reminding me that we all have a kid inside of us and we shouldn't always take life so seriously. My most heartfelt thanks go to my wife, Chelle, for her ongoing support and for being patient with me as I was working on this manuscript. I also want to thank her for her fabulous pictures, which are featured exclusively throughout this book. Finally, I would like to thank God, without whom I would not have the talents that I have.

Important Note
This pet owner's manual tells the reader how to buy or adopt, and care for a Puggle. The author and publisher consider it important to point out that the advice given in the book is meant primarily for normally developed dogs of excellent physical health and sound temperament.

Anyone who acquires a fully grown dog should be aware that the animal has already formed its basic impressions of human beings. The new owner should observe the animal carefully, including its behavior toward humans, and, whenever possible, should meet the previous owner.

Caution is further advised in the association of children with dogs, in meeting with other dogs, and in exercising the dog without a leash.

Even well-behaved and carefully supervised dogs can sometimes damage property or cause accidents. It is therefore in the owner's interest to be adequately insured against such eventualities, and we strongly urge all dog owners to purchase a liability policy that also covers their dog.

About the Author
Andre Calbert is the president of the Northern California–based Designerdoggies.com, an organization dedicated to educating the public and furthering the recognition of hybrid dogs. His organization also provides a well-known puppy finder service as well as hybrid rescues. He has been featured in many prestigious newspaper and magazines articles around the globe for his knowledge on the subject and has also done talk radio and television spots. Calbert has many projects in development, including a Weblog, a hybrid dog show, and a television show. Andre has personally handled and cared for hundreds of Puggles, both puppies and adults, and is a known expert on the breed.

All inquiries should be addressed to:
Barron's Educational Series, Inc.
250 Wireless Boulevard
Hauppauge, NY 11788
www.barronseduc.com

ISBN-13: 978-0-7641-3662-7
ISBN-10: 0-7641-3662-3

Library of Congress Catalog Card No. 2007005009

Library of Congress Cataloging-in-Publication Data
Calbert, Andre.
    Puggles : everything about purchase, care,
    nutrition, behavior, and training / Andre Calbert ;
    filled with full-color photographs be Chelle Calbert.
        p. cm.
    Includes Index.
    ISBN-13: 978-0-7641-3662-7
    ISBN-10: 0-7641-3662-3
    1. Puggle.

SF429.P92 C35   2007
636.76—dc22   2007005009

Printed in China
9 8 7 6 5 4 3 2 1